T0067189

Lines
of Listening

**An Expose' of Generational
Child Abuse and Marital Betrayal**

Joyce K. Gatschenberger

authorHOUSE®

AuthorHouse™
1663 Liberty Drive
Bloomington, IN 47403
www.authorhouse.com
Phone: 1 (800) 839-8640

© 2015 Joyce K. Gatschenberger. All rights reserved.

No part of this book may be reproduced, stored in a retrieval system, or transmitted by any means without the written permission of the author.

Published by AuthorHouse   10/16/2015

ISBN: 978-1-5049-3374-2 (sc)
ISBN: 978-1-5049-3373-5 (e)

Library of Congress Control Number: 2015916070

Print information available on the last page.

Any people depicted in stock imagery provided by Thinkstock are models, and such images are being used for illustrative purposes only. Certain stock imagery © Thinkstock.

This book is printed on acid-free paper.

Because of the dynamic nature of the Internet, any web addresses or links contained in this book may have changed since publication and may no longer be valid. The views expressed in this work are solely those of the author and do not necessarily reflect the views of the publisher, and the publisher hereby disclaims any responsibility for them.

This book is dedicated to my granddaughter, Kiyah Doveanna.
I wrote it so that she can learn about, and truly know,
her family and herself.

Contents

Foreword

Lines of Listening is a collection of life memories. Often, I tell my children about their grandparents and extended family. Sometimes, I apologize for an unintentional wrong. Occasionally, I explain things and situations that I don't understand. Mostly, I place feelings, thoughts, and memories into words that tell the story of my life from my perspective. If others were to relate their thoughts about these events, they may have a different view, something more to their liking. It wouldn't be my thoughts, my perspective, though. This is my story.

Lines of Listening is also a conversation about the people and events in my life that shaped my destiny. Sometimes, I listen to these conversations and enjoy them, sometimes not. Often, they are persistent, idle chatter buzzing around in my head, which I try to ignore. Frequently, they give me grief. Usually, they offer great challenges to me. Sometimes, they are annoying because I don't like what they say. However, I can't deny that they all shaped my life. I try to relate them honestly. At times, the *lines* are strong, and the influence is intense. Occasionally, the *lines* are weak and barely visible to the naked eye; they pass through my life as if they were a delicate far off whisper-yet they leave a *line* that lasts a lifetime.

Recognizing that my mother gave me a gift is simple. I refer to it often in this book. It's the double-edged sword of stubbornness. She got it from her mother, who in turn, got it from her mother. It helps me survive through difficult situations. It keeps me motivated in times of great trials. It helps me complete tasks, which I never dreamed possible. Sometimes, it gets me in trouble. But mostly it helps me to heal my scars and get on with the business of life. There is a saying among the robust women in my family, "there are no quitters in our family." It is repeated to each of us when things get tough and things are often tough. As Mary Karr relates in her book *The Liars' Club,* "a dysfunctional family is any family with more than one person in it."

Also in this writing you will find how I view the difference between the words "hearing" and "listening." We are all capable of *hearing* sounds around us every day if we have the anatomical equipment in our ear canal and it is working correctly. But I am not talking about how our bodies are sensitive to vibrations of noise that enter our ears' range of detection. In this book, I focused on what we as humans do with the noises that we detect. During verbal conversations between people, the non-verbal juxtaposed interactions often reveal the true essence of the conversation (i.e. clenched teeth while saying "I love you"). [1] This true essence is listening, in my opinion, and it is the difference between *hearing* and *listening.* The converted message implanted into our psychological radar is permanently imprinted. It is what forms the schematic of our selves. What we decide to do with the noise that enters into our realm of detection and how we, as individuals, consciously or unconsciously file this information into streams of belief, molds who we are and determines the manner in which we deal with the matters that occur in life. [2]

This is the premise that builds the *Lines of Listening.* The pathway for this premise is set up in our lives from our very beginning-possibly even before we are born into this world. Scientific studies have indicated that the fetus is influenced by sounds and activities both inside and outside the body prior to birth. When a mother drops a metal pot or pan on a hard tile floor with a loud clang, the fetus will show signs of being startled by flexing body muscles or moving away from the noise. This action could be a positive coping strategy and may be an example of a fetus developing its *Lines of Listening* in the womb. Also, in my research as a nurse for the past thirty years, I have noted that when a pregnant woman is subjected to intense stress, her body will release hormones in response to that stress. This observation was verified by a prominent perinatologist who is the director of maternal-fetal medicine at Cedar Sinai Medical Center and a professor

---

[1] Burley-Allen, M. (1995) Listening: The forgotten skill: A self-teaching guide (2nd Ed.). New York: John Wiley and Sons, Inc.

[2] Goulston, M. D. & Ferrazzi, K. (2009) Just listen: Discover the secret to getting through to absolutely anyone.
New York: AMACOM.

obstetrics/gynecology and pediatrics at the University of California at Los Angeles. He showed that stress was not good for pregnant women.[3]

Further research indicates that parents need to be conscious of how they manage the noise in their children's lives. Often, when a parent is unable to manage harmful noises in a child's environment, the child learns to develop inappropriate, adaptive strategies to cope with the irritating vibrations. This suggests that even very young children are sensitive to noise in their environment. In a book entitled *Facilitating Hearing and Listening in Young Children*, Carol Flexor, Ph.D., relates that both hearing sensitivity and a focused listening environment are crucial for a young child's audibility development, the ability to detect speech, and intelligibility development, the ability to discriminate between words and sounds.[4] *Lines of Listening* is an account of how I became aware of the noise that I was hearing and what I chose to do when I listened to that noise.

You will discover that I listened often to the noise of my childhood. However, I regret that in reviewing the relationships I have had with my ancestral family, I discovered that I have a scant library of actual conversations with people. There was value in taking time, within the busy context of life, to sit and to talk with the elders in my family in order to retrieve the family history hidden away in their memories. This proves to be a handicap when I attempt to write down my own life experiences. My memories may well differ from the reality of situations that occurred in the past.

Therefore, I decided to share my writings with my children as they are being set to paper. Sometimes they want to listen, sometimes they ask about the progress of my work. Often they are also too busy to understand the vintage value of my words. I am hopeful that history will preserve my writings for them to read later in their life when their ears are ready to hear.

---

[3] WebMD (2014) Fetus to mom: You're stressing me out. Retrieved from www. webmd.com December 21, 2014..

[4] Flexer, C. (1999) Facilitating hearing and listening in young children. New York: Delmar Cengage Learning.

Chapter 1

Ancestors

My ancestral history travels through the war-torn fields of Germany, toward immigration into the United States and finally, successful settlement in the bucolic towns of the Midwest. I'm familiar with my father's stoic, Germanic family but my mother's equally intense heritage is more fleeting.

This record is only a bit of my ancestry, the small portion which impacts me. However, I savor the struggle that my extended family endured to ensure a life in which I could decide my own future. I was born and raised in a cocoon of impervious and abused individuals who ignored any need to relive past family deeds and interactions. The adults of my extended family securely kept their silent ancestral history. They shielded our past and the previous abusive struggles of my family. However, I owe all that I am to my DNA that has struggled before me.

The Merriam-Webster Dictionary lists an ancestor as "one from whom an individual is descended." I knew that I, just as most people, had ancestors. However, it was as if once my extended family and I were transported to this bucolic Midwestern setting, we pretended that our past history and family life were non-existent. Of interest to me was that my father's mothers' family and my father's fathers' family lived within a few miles of each other in the town where I grew up, and yet, I never saw them together. In fact, it wasn't until I was in high school that I realized my paternal grandfather's family lived in the same community. It was then that I gave in to the nagging of my inner radar and investigated how

I happened to be born in this particular city at this particular time with these particular people.

The book entitled, *The Stieren Family* (my paternal grandmother), published by an extended family member outlines a portion of our family's journey from Germany to the United States.[5] She related that my ancestors had migrated into the "land of freedom" in order to escape compulsory military service and to expand abilities in the mining and farming professions.

Another ancestor, still living in Germany, informed me that my paternal great-great grandfather, Simon Gatschenberger (1670-1741) - Ludwig's father - was a man who fathered fifteen children by three wives - tracing that part of the family remains unfinished and perhaps sketchy.

In order to gain a fuller knowledge of my ancestors and to understand why my parents, aunts, and uncles interacted with each other as they did, I needed to know about my family before I was born. The question that weighed on me was, primarily, "Why did my parents behave so badly?" The struggle to answer this amidst the silence of those closest to me prompted me to research my ancestors - the Stieren and Gatschenberger families. I both thank them and curse them for my linage.

****

The *Stieren* family records begin in West Germany in Badem - the village situated in the Eifel region of the Rhineland. It was there that the *Stammhaus* or the ancestral home was built. This village was defenseless due to its geographic location, and, as a result, it became a place of abuse, torture, and murder. At times, the citizens were tracked down with bloodhounds to the very last man—the only survivors fled to the hills. Many residents lived in caves and foxholes. These hill people were my distant relatives. However, the village itself remained unpopulated until 1656, when a few of those in hiding returned to it. In 1659, the diocese of Bitburg recorded only 17 homes.[6]

---

[5]   Weitekamp, L. (1986) Stieren family of Badem, West Germany, 1618-1986. Illinois: NSDAR.

[6]   Ibid.

In the 18th century, this area experienced upward development. Within three to four generations the population multiplied immensely and, by 1790, totaled nearly 400 people. During the Napoleonic Wars under Napoleon I, France had looted the land that would become Germany. Otto Eduard Leopold von Bismarck, the Chancellor of the North German Confederation wanted a united nation but knew that the Protestant northern states and the Catholic southern states were culturally divided on more than just religion. However, Bismarck recognized they could agree on one thing–their hatred of France. To get the war started, Bismarck flung insults at the French that Napoleon III could not allow.

The resulting Franco-Prussian War (1870-71) had a profound effect on my German-born ancestors. Germany was swift in its use of the latest in war technology and railroads to defeat and capture Napoleon III and his army. However, that war, like any other, had a lasting and permanent negative effect on my father's maternal grandfather. Like so many other soldiers, he saw the horrors of death and dismemberment that befell his fellow comrades. He physically survived but swore an oath: None of his sons or descendents would ever fight in so horrible a conflict. He completed his compulsory duty in the Prussian Army and vowed that his sons would never pledge allegiance to the abhorrent Prussian state. Wilheim Stieren began immediate preparations to move his young family to America.

Although Wilhelm emigrated, proof of our ancestral roots remains today in the Village of Badem at the intersection of Bundesstrasse and Kirchstrasse. There you will find a tall cross marked with the inscription "1703—Stiren Theis von Badem" and a pair of scissors denoting that this man was a tailor. (Stieren Family Hx – Linda Weitekamp – Sherman, IL.) Whatever the Stieren family did before their departure from Germany, however, had some effect on what they did once they arrived in America.

****

It is 1883. William (Wilhelm) Stieren, at the age of 38, had finally saved enough for a trip to the U.S.A. and arrived in Spaulding, Illinois after sailing from Saarbrucken in what is now West Germany.[7] He had

---

[7]   Ibid.

been married to Katharina (Catherine) Wilhelmina Holzer for eleven years. He had few marketable skills but decided to make a living through coal mining. By this time in American history, it was becoming an industrialized profession, and William was eager to profit in it.

William, and his brother Leonard, had initially learned the craft in Germany while subsidizing their income through part-time work on a small farm in Altenwald (a suburb of Saarbrucken). Their sweat and toil made it possible for the brothers to earn a meager wage that enabled them to earn passage for the United States in 1883. They believed this land offered a more promising outlook for their families. It was the last time either of them would ever again see their homeland. Their hope was to establish a home for their families while establishing themselves in the coal mining business. They settled in Spalding, Illinois because of its well-known coal mining industry.

Wilhelm's wife, Katharina, and their five children did not come with the brothers initially. Instead, they secured overseas passage six months later. They had to sell all of their personal belongings in order to buy enough food for the trip.

I have often thought about this experience and wondered if I could sell all of my worldly possessions in order to follow a dream for my family. Could I give up everything I owned on the chance that I might make a better life in another place? Obviously, the Stieren family knew it would be a one-way trip. Records indicate that when Wilhelm and Katharina arrived in the United States each of their first names were changed in an attempt to Americanize them: Wilhelm to William and Katharina to Catherine. Not only had they lost their homeland but they were in danger of losing their individual identity as well. Again, I question if I would have been able to do the same.

The living quarters on the ship for Catherine and her children were so cramped that there was only one bed for her and the children to share. When Catherine would lie down, the girls would lie sideways across her legs. Occasionally, her legs would cramp, the girls would have to stand so she could relieve the cramps. During this difficult voyage, Catherine was caring for five young children: Magdalena (my paternal grandmother age 11), Sophie (9), Karl (4), William (2), and an infant son, Hermann. Another son, also named William, had died in Germany before the family left for

America. I can only image how intense a long ocean bound voyage would be especially in such extremely cramped quarters with small children.

My cousin, Linda W, related a piece of our family story that I had never heard. Catherine's infant son, Hermann, was born after William's departure for America. Due to his young age, the infant became very ill on the voyage. At one point, Catherine believed he was dead. She wrapped the baby very tightly in a blanket so that there would be no detectable odor, determined that her husband would see his son even if he were dead. When the authorities came to check on the passengers, she begged them not to wake the baby because he was ill, and she had just put him to sleep. She knew that if they discovered that he was dead, they would insist on burying him at sea. When the ship arrived in port and she checked the infant, she discovered that he was indeed still alive. Unfortunately, he remained in poor health and later died at the age of nine.

I can only imagine the heartbreak she must have endured during the voyage. To suffer such physical hardships in addition to the emotional hardships of losing a child while being the caregiver, provider, and protector for her other children must have be strenuous to say the least. There was no plan "B." I'm positive that she was not only terrified but also cautious during every long moment of the ocean voyage.

In total, William and Catherine had ten children. In addition to the five who traveled to America with Catherine and the one who died in Germany, they had two daughters who died in infancy after Catherine arrived in America The heartache must have been great for both parents to endure the loss of young children so soon after their trip to America. Later, Louis was born in 1887, and Mary Cecelia was born in 1890.

I didn't discover any information or record to indicate that either William or Catherine learned to speak English before setting out on their trip. It is highly likely that they both had to deal with and function in a world where the language, customs, routines, and laws were foreign and potentially frightening to them. One example of the culture shock this must have caused is a family story about the day that Catherine and the children arrived in Springfield, Illinois. William was unable to take time off of work from the mines. Therefore, he sent a black man in a wagon with a handwritten note to the train station for Catherine and the children. In the note, he explained that this person would take them to their new home.

Young William, who was about four years old, had never seen a black person before in his life. Therefore, William refused to get into the wagon. Catherine pulled him into the wagon without taking his protests into account. He promptly jumped off the wagon and ran, crying and screaming, through the train station depot. He was finally captured and made to sit in back of the wagon for the ride to their new home. I can imagine that young William was terrified the entire time since he had to sit next to a person who spoke a different language and looked very different from anyone that he had ever seen before.

There is no indication from my family history research that my German-born ancestors came from aristocratic stock. Records reveal a hard-working, truthful, God-fearing, family-oriented people, possessing a burning desire to improve the living conditions of their family.

They arrived in America during a time of intense growth. The moguls of their time, the Vanderbilt's, the Carnegie's, the Rockefeller's, the Morgan's, and the Westinghouse's, were in the midst of a constant struggle to monopolize the industrialization of the United States. During a twenty-year growth explosion between the 1880's and 1900's, these tycoons of oil, railroad, electricity, commerce, and interstate trade were in the midst of a paradigm shift that was priming the United States to become one of the most powerful countries on earth. In the last twenty years of the 19th century, the population of major cities in the United States jumped to fifteen million persons. America was economically and commercially moving forward.

It was obvious that if a person or family were to succeed in this environment, they would need to assimilate to their new home quickly and use the new technology to their benefit. William and Catherine knew this and quickly began putting their talents to work as a team. William and his brothers worked in the coalmines during the day and in the family orchards in the evening. Catherine and the older children would tend the fields and orchards during their waking hours and then transport their wares to the public market for sale.

William and Catherine were soon able to buy a small farm in Spalding, Illinois. They raised fruits and vegetables, selling them at the local produce markets. Aunt Mayme told me about a general store/tavern located on Cook Street in Springfield, Illinois. It was there where William and

Catherine sold their produce and was also where my paternal grandmother, Magdalena (William and Catherine's oldest daughter), met my paternal grandfather (Otto Joseph Gatschenberger). This building was demolished in November of 1999.

William and his brother Leonard worked at the Lincoln Park Coal and Brick Company mine across from the Oak Ridge Cemetery. A cousin told me that even young William, who was four years old when he came to the United States with his mother, went to work in the mines with his father and uncle by the time he was in the third grade. I don't know why such a young child was subjected to this servitude other than to add financial support to the family coffers. It is overwhelming to me that each family member keenly felt the burden of securing his or her success.

I wonder if William was greatly distressed when his young son joined him in that lifelong profession of backbreaking labor. Or possibly, he believed that he was teaching his young son a profession that would bring him a lifelong source of income. Whatever the reason, young William spent most of his childhood years working beside his uncle and father in the Illinois coalmines.

To illustrate the financial difficulties that must have occurred at that time, I offer you the story of Hermann, the sickly infant on the sea crossing. He died in 1893, and the bill for burying Herman in Calvary Cemetery cost William and Catherine $5.00. William didn't have the money to pay for it and had to borrow the funds from the local butcher. Despite the intense personal sorrow my ancestor must have been going through, he was forced to solicit funds from the only available local ethnic bank for the group of families who had settled in this area. One can assume it was expected that if a family was in need, the butcher was the institution that would loan the funds to them. Knowing that my great-grandfather didn't have the money to bury his son simply highlights the intense sacrifice that my ancestors endured in order to ensure that our family would be successful in the United States.

This surely was an emotionally trying situation for my great-grandparents. I often wonder if I have the same fortitude and grit that inhabited them. They seemed to be able to bear and overcome intense obstacles both mentally and physically to settle into Illinois society. Would I be able to make the trip to a foreign country with my family? Would I be able to swallow my pride and approach the local butcher to request funds in order to pay for the burial of my young child? I wonder. Obviously, my forefathers were filled with tenacity, perseverance, hardiness, self-will, and stubbornness. These are all characteristics that served them well in forging a new life in the New World.

In reading documents of our family history, it appears that many other immigrant families from Germany tended to work and thrive in closed communities (as did other immigrant ethnic groups). I'm sure being surrounded by people from a similar culture offered comfort and security while they acclimatized to the new country. People within this community shared the same language and struggles learning that new language. In reviewing a family history book compiled by my older cousin, I discovered other German families immigrated to the United States at this time and settled in this area. She informed me that one of these immigrants was a blacksmith named Mike Raylots, who worked at the Lincoln Park mine with my relatives. He later married Sophie Stieren, my grandmother's sister.

Chapter 2

The Sisters, Three

It's March 15, 1969. Having celebrated my twentieth birthday last week, I am celebrating my marriage today. I'm dwarfed at the base of the stairs below the baroque altar of a Catholic Church in Springfield, Illinois - my childhood church. Standing in my hand-made wedding gown, the ornately adorned priest pronounces me "Mrs." - forever. I tentatively turn to face the congregation while grasping my husband's hand and begin the lifelong walk down the aisle of matrimonial bliss.

As I parade down the spectator-lined aisle, I briefly glance out of the corner of my eye and catch the unison nod of the aunts - three of my father's older sisters who, from all family accounts, were responsible for raising him to adulthood. It's just a slight tilt of their heads – not really noticeable to the casual observer. It's a brief encounter, but it gives a lifetime of permission. It informs me that I can let go and live my life. I can make my own history. This is the last time that I will see the Sisters, Three: Aunt Mayme, the keeper of family secrets, Aunt Sophia, the meek seamstress, and Aunt Catherine, the authoritarian.

I'm certain that youth once visited the sisters. Surely, supple skin graced their young, flexible bodies. However, I wonder: *how did those three non-assuming, elderly, wizened women with their slumping shoulders and wrinkle-bearing faces, in richly adorned yet antiquated clothing become simply three invisible women?*

****

A brief honeymoon trip signaled decades of traveling the country as a military wife - raising a family of my own. However, my thoughts often drifted back to the family stories related to me by the Sisters, Three. They had begrudgingly liberated the tightly guarded ancestral history only after much urging. They relinquished tidbits of family confidences only when their mental and psychological guard was relaxed. I am sure that even though I was lucky enough to receive momentary glimpses into my ancestors past, there were a lot of things that, to this day, remain secretly cloaked, things that have gone to the grave with my aunts and uncles.

As I write this, my father and all of his twelve brothers and sisters have passed away. The three oldest sisters left some sketchy memories and a few faded pictures tucked away in dusty scrapbooks from which I have had to nudge a legacy for my family.

According to our family verbal history - the Sisters, Three were the driving force in my father's survival. They were the protective bastions for their younger siblings against the drunken raging beatings of my paternal grandfather. They had sheltered their younger siblings when grandpa brought home his girlfriends and continually soiled his marriage bed despite my grandmother's repeated, pleading protests.

However, these were only bits and pieces of the oral history that narrated their early entry into the adult burden of childrearing for their younger siblings. Their tender years were scarred by the yoke of caring for their increasingly fragile mother. She gave birth to ten additional children after marrying Otto Joseph Gatschenberger, and my father was the thirteenth child that she bore. By all accounts, his birth was especially difficult, and my grandmother's health never recovered. Aunt Mayme related stories of how she particularly nurtured my father - becoming his primary caregiver.

Aunt Mayme told me that my grandfather operated a successful truck farm, and it was important that all of the produce, which had so tenderly been grown to maturity, made it to market so that it could be sold for a profit. A truck farm is where a farmer grows local produce, such as corn, tomatoes, potatoes, beans, asparagus, peas, and assorted fruits, and then trucks them (i.e. ships them via small trucks or wagons) to local stores in order to sell them to local residents.

As a very young child, my father was repeatedly tethered to a pole in my paternal grandfather's greenhouse at night to guard it. These oral rumors, these bits of verbal memories, were the tidbits that mentally nudged my curiosity about our genealogy into unraveling our shared history.

****

It is October, 1890, 53-year old Ludwig and 43-year old Maria (Lell) Gatschenberger, my paternal great-grandparents, immigrate to America from Katzendahl (a suburb of Badem), Germany. They are accompanied by their daughter, 22-year old Anna, and their third child, 17-year old Otto Joseph - who became my paternal grandfather(see picture of German passport). They endure a lengthy and uncertain ocean voyage on a ship named *EMS*. This ship sailing on Lake Simcoe ferries other ethnic families searching for new lives in America.

Otto's brother, Benedict Joseph, the first-born son, came to America in 1888 to establish a footprint for the family in the United States. He was lucky to find employment as a police officer in the Illinois area. Benedict's lineage is short. After marrying Mary Lehnen, he died July 2, 1945 in Springfield, IL. – childless. Likewise, Anna married a citizen of Springfield – John Theisen, but they also had no children.

In fact, only Ludwig's youngest child, Otto Joseph, had children to carry on the family's heritage.

After four short years of intense struggle and sacrifice in the land of opportunity, Ludwig died in Springfield at the age of 57. Maria outlived him by more than two decades and died in Springfield at the age of 69. Again, this research line was revealed only after internet and archived newspaper searching.

****

It's March 2, 1897. John H. Lueschen has just died, leaving Magdelena Francis (Stieren) Lueschen a 24-year old widow with three young daughters: four-year old Catherine, three-year old Mary, and one-year old Sophia.7 These Sisters, Three were known to me as Aunt Catherine, Aunt Mayme, and Aunt Sophie. There is no record of Magdelena having any marketable skills such as typing, office management, nursing, or other "appropriate" female-oriented business training. Magdelena married Otto Joseph Gatschenberger on May 17, 1899, after two years of supporting three young daughters in unknown ways. At that point, she may have felt that marriage was her only option, or she may have fallen deeply in love with my Grandfather Gatschenberger. I don't know for certain, and the Sisters, Three never talked about their relationship. I was only able to glean hints about it by listening to the sketchy verbal stories the sisters so begrudgingly related.

If my grandparents initially formed a union of affection, Otto's demands of strict obedience and many children seems to have quickly cooled any amorous interaction that may have existed. Nine years after arriving in America, Otto had a family and was an independent businessman. During the next fourteen years, Magdelena gave birth to ten more children. My father, William Charles, was the youngest.

The oral family history states that Catherine, Mayme, and Sophie were never formally adopted by my grandfather. That I could find no record of a formal adoption seems to support that. Each picture I have of the Sisters, Three shows them standing together with bodies touching as if in a huddled, protective position. I have to wonder if it's a stance developed throughout their lifetimes to ward off external threats, either real or imagined. However, that is something no one will ever know. The Sisters, Three were very dubious about sharing any family history concerning their childhood. The bits and pieces I was able to coax from them seemed to lack happy or joyful memories.

According to local Springfield, IL newspaper clippings and the 1902 edition of Polk's Springfield City Directory, Otto Joseph was a multi-talented man. He worked as a local constable, produce farmer, sheriff, and saloonkeeper. I'm sure that this was an interesting balancing act. One thing my aunts did agree on is that my grandfather ran a very productive alcohol still. His saloon was located at 1901 East Cook St., and a large portion of the family's support came from bootlegging. Since he is also listed as a sheriff for the Sangamon County area during a time when prohibition was beginning to attract much support, one has to wonder how he managed to walk on both sides of the law. From what I have learned about the man,

I doubt that my grandfather had any worries about these two professions coexisting as long as each of them brought in money.

Otto Joseph's greenhouse and nursery were situated next to his residence at 1918 East Cook. The Polk's Springfield City Directory for 1902 also lists Otto Joseph's children, Anna, Benjamin (a miner), and Mary (Aunt Mayme) (a housekeeper), as living at 1914 East Cook Street. The truck farm seemed to have been another of the family's sources of income.

Aunt Mayme related stories concerning how my paternal grandparents initially met in my grandfather's produce market. Magdelena's family would deliver and sell produce from their fruit orchard at Otto's store/saloon. It was common in those days for families involved in businesses and of similar ethnic groups (i.e. German grocers, German miners, etc.) to know and interact with each other on a daily basis. The men would often work together, and the women probably shared in the tedious household and gardening duties.

Otto and Magdelena married and moved into 1918 East Cook Street. Since Otto never officially adopted Catherine, Mary (Mayme) and Sophie, their official last name remained Lueschen. However, documents, such as a local census and the 1900 United States Federal Census, interchange their last name between Getshanburger (Gatschenberger) and Lueschen. The ten additional children created during Magdelena and Otto's marriage were: Anna, Helen, Christian, Otto Joseph, Ludwig, Magdalena, Benedict Joseph, John Joseph, Clara Louise, and William Charles. Only seven of these children survived to adulthood.

Reviewing family photos, I located a faded picture of one deceased daughter, Clara Louise. It was taken when she was fifteen years old. She looks sad and pensive but was truly a natural beauty. Just from looking at Aunt Clara's picture, I feel that I would have liked her if I would have had the opportunity to know her.

Four years later, when she was about nineteen years old, she met with a brutal fate. She was brutally gang raped by a couple of young, neighborhood men. By all family members' accounts, it was a vicious attack. According to Aunt Helen and Aunt Mayme, my uncles carried her battered and bruised body to the nearest medical facility, which happened to be a dental office. She received only basic medical care from the dentist.

However, her injuries were so serious that she couldn't be moved to a hospital. By all accounts, she died a painful death at a tender, innocent age.

As soon as they finished caring for Clara Louise, my uncles took several weapons and chased down her attackers. An extensive search revealed the rapists, who had to have known they would be served up "country justice by the boys." They were beaten so severely that they also died.

With my grandfather as the Springfield sheriff, it should come as no surprise to learn that no charges were ever filed against my uncles. My grandfather was well known to carry a pistol in one hand and a jug of whiskey in the other. There is documentation showing that he delivered the law "as he saw fit."

Whenever I reflect on the Sisters, Three, I am reminded of their reluctance to share the stories of their childhood. It must have been a brutal, dysfunctional family arrangement having a conflicting father who was officially a representative of the law but who had no concern for the law. Developing children need loving, nurturing, and hope-providing guidance to advance through their lives into strong, productive, self-supporting adults. Obviously, my aunts and uncles did not receive any of these emotional or psychological tools. Instead, they were prepared for a world of hate and abuse and forced to develop skills of self-preservation and defense.

I am saddened when I think of it. I know that there must have been potential for our family to be a close, loving, and protective unit–the potential that exists for any family–but any chance was destroyed. I have to wonder if there was something intense and harmful in Otto's past that scarred him forever–something that prevented him from showing love and tenderness to his wife and children. I wonder if his father was harsh and harmful to him during his formative years. These are things that I will never know. What I do know is that all my aunts, uncles, and father carried the psychological scars of abuse and neglect throughout their adult lives.

Even as a small child I detected the feelings of sadness and unworthiness projected from them. My father treated my mother, siblings, and myself badly. He was an unhappy and angry man until his death. Even when they were adults, the Sisters, Three always seemed to instinctively huddle around each other as though they were protecting themselves from an ever-present danger.

****

My first memory of Aunt Catherine, the oldest of the thirteen children, was when I was about three or four years old. I went with my dad and older sister, LaJean, to visit her. The house was on the rich side of town, and it took a long drive to get there. When my dad stopped the car, I got out but stopped in my tracks. Before me was the most beautiful castle I had ever seen. I remember thinking that I had never seen such a beautiful house. It was enormous: at least two or three stories high and embedded with sparkles and colored glass trim.

My dad had forewarned me not to act up at Aunt Catherine's house. If I did, I knew I would receive a harsh, physical beating when we returned home. I stood statue still, waiting with him and my sister at the massive front door while my father knocked. Shortly, I heard heavy, determined footsteps. A matronly, no- nonsense woman finally opened it. She greeted my dad with familiarity, touching his shoulder and smiling at him.

She led us to the front room, but we paused after entering it only a few steps.

The woman bent down so that her face was square with mine.

"You go over there and keep Uncle Nick company," She said, pointing her bony, whitewashed finger to a dark corner at the far side of the room. My eyes involuntarily squinted and tried to focus on the object where she was pointing. Slowly, I realized that the distant form was a slump-shouldered man dressed in a well-adorned red and purple robe. He was positioned in a wooden chair with wheels on each side of it. "Just sit on the bench. Don't touch anything, and don't bother him." I did as I was told without hesitation.

As I sat in the dark, quiet room with this strange man, my mind filled with questions. *"Why had Aunt Catherine referred to this person, whom I had never previously met, as uncle? Who was he?"*

I learned later from my mother that Aunt Catherine had been a private duty nurse and had taken care of wealthy people in their homes. She had cared for Nicholas Amrhein's wife before she died. After his wife died, he became a widower with five children. He married Aunt Catherine on May 9, 1936.

After many moments of relentless, unspoken questions filling my mind, I realized that I was alone in the dark room with a scary old man who I didn't know, and he was sitting in a creepy chair. My sister and dad had disappeared. This place was dark, smelled badly, and was frightening. I didn't realize it at the time, but I now believe that my aunt saw this as the perfect place for me: hidden and out of the way.

Thankfully, I had already learned this lesson: I could withstand anything. My parents used physical, powerful beatings to teach it to me. I learned early that I had no protector; I could never show weakness; I could never show pain. Whatever emotion raged within, I needed to deal with it inside and not let anyone know that I was really a warm, feeling, loving, soft, intelligent human being. I may have been young, but I was stubborn. This was just another training ground for so many similar scenes throughout my life.

Suddenly, I was jolted back into reality by a strong, sweet smell integrating into the musky room. It was originating from the crack under the door of the closed kitchen: the delicious smell of homemade chocolate chip cookies.

I suddenly realized that my aunt, my sister, and my father were all in the kitchen eating freshly baked cookies, which Aunt Catherine must have just taken out of the oven. I couldn't believe it!

I may have been only three or four years old, but I certainly felt the sting of rejection. In my mind, the message blared loud and clear: I was a chubby child and didn't need any cookies. Prior to this time, I suspected I was not the favorite– especially in Aunt Catherine's eyes. Now I knew my place in the family for sure! I could see Aunt Catherine's pleasure in knowing that I was just inches outside the door but could not be part of the party.

In that one instant, that scent held the key that unlocked the hidden secret of my unworthiness. It condemned me to my designated place in the family structure. All I could do was focus on the message. The swinging door to the kitchen was closed, but the faint scent of chocolate drifted through the crack along with soft voices from behind the door. The longer they stayed in the segregated sanctuary, the louder their voices became. The chosen-ones were in the kitchen enjoying their celebration, and I wasn't invited!

Left to myself with only a feeble, quiet, strange man as comfort, I allowed my rage to build. I knew that I was not the male child my father wanted. He had made that clear in so many ways through everyday actions and slights. Despite my young age, I had already become self-conscience of my weight. As I sat, an outcast from the camaraderie, in a dark, creepy, musty room with a scary, old man that I didn't know, I decided to pretend that nothing was wrong. I fought back the moist droplets that battled so desperately to fill my eyes. I would not let them win. I would not let them reveal my feelings of betrayal. I avoided my unknown uncle–I could not let anyone look into my eyes. I had been wounded, but I refused to admit my weakness to anyone.

From an even earlier age, I learned that the punishment for showing weakness or emotion, except anger, in my family was ridicule and humiliation. I had good teachers on this matter, my dysfunctional family. However, in this short time in my aunt's front room, the desire to release the pain of my depreciation was great. For the rest of my life, my inner voice screamed the mantra it learned at this moment,

"I am not worthy. I am not the chosen one." That this one moment affected me for the rest of my life is tribute to the emotional damage it had done. Even as an adult, the scent of a chocolate chip cookie can force me to relive this demeaning moment again and again.

I kept my eyes and ears open. Repeatedly, I found evidence that not only Aunt Catherine, Aunt Mayme, and Aunt Sophie looked at me differently, but also all my dads' brothers and sisters. They never told me with their words but they certainly screamed with their actions, "What a poor, little, fat girl." Family functions were only more stressful as I wondered if they were secretly laughing at me or pitying me. In my mind, I could hear their whispers, "Gee, she could be pretty if she just wasn't so fat."

I didn't find one family member to protect and support me. There weren't confidants to bear my soul. All I had was myself. To further alienate me, it seemed as if my older sister did find support from others in my family. So much was the support for her, that in my mind I began calling her the "chosen child." Little examples of the preferential treatment (beyond the episode with the cookies) stand out in my mind.

I remember when she first left home in her teen years under very strained circumstances. By this time, the Sisters, Three were living together on Ninth Street. If my memory is not playing tricks on me, they had an addition to their house built to accommodate her. She had a large bedroom, a private bath, and a separate entrance that allowed her to come and go at her convenience. Aunt Sophie made her clothes. Aunt Mayme made meals for her when she came home from work each day. I watched this arrangement from a distance in awe and amazement. For whatever reason, the Sisters, Three had decided to protect and nurture my sister in the same way they must have protected and cared for my father when he was young.

Years later, another episode of favoritism occurred when my older sister wanted to buy into an ice cream franchise. This time, the Sisters, Three urged Magdalena Gatschenberger-Weber, or Aunt Pat as we called her, to give my sister a very large sum of money for that purpose. When the business ultimately failed, my sister never had to account for the money or to repay it. To the best of my knowledge, it was never mentioned again.

There were many times when the rest of us could have used such a generous gift, but there was never any mention of a similar act of kindness. From my point of view, the Sisters, Three would watch out for my older sister and protect her, but that same privilege was not afforded to her siblings.

****

I have other early childhood memories of the Sisters, Three. It was only a couple of years after the chocolate chip cookie incident that Uncle Nicholas died. At that point, Aunt Catherine and her disabled daughter, Joann, moved into the big house on Ninth Street with Aunt Mayme and Aunt Sophie. Once they moved in together, my dad would drive my siblings and me over to their grand two-story house on Ninth Street to visit.

Their well-manicured street was impressive. All the houses in the neighborhood were painted white with shuttered windows trimmed in dark green. Front yard flower garden paths were tended by contracted gardeners. The houses were edged by driveways that folded around to the back and ended in wood framed garages.

18

When my dad came to a stop, we would noisily ramble out of the car and run up to the bottom of the cement stairs like all children. However, there we would abruptly stop, verbally halted by my dads' command. As the mood shifted to somber watchfulness, we knew that only old people lived here. Despite our youth, we had to be old people while we visited. We knew this meant we were not allowed to make noise or to touch anything.

From the moment we entered, the house had the smell and feel of old people. Even the air was old. The air inside the house never got stirred around or moved. None of the new, outside air was welcome inside to be mixed up with what was already there. Not only was I expected to follow act old, but also I couldn't disturb the air in the house without bringing trouble on myself.

I knew that I could not act up. I had to be quiet and walk through the halls and rooms without jumping or talking loud. Once, when I forgot momentarily where I was, I ran down the front hallway. All the fine china figurines in the glass case by the door rattled. Aunt Catherine came out of the back kitchen like a bull. She headed straight in my direction, tightened up her face, lowered her head so that her eyes were even with mine, and said – *"don't ever run in here."* I never did it again.

It seemed as if Aunt Catherine always had rules for me, which contributed to my feelings of isolation. I never saw her smile or laugh. She never even tried to hide her strong dislike for me. On the rare occasions when she felt it necessary to inform me of yet another command or rule, she stared down at me, tightened her lips, and pointed her finger in my face while she did it. In fact, she greeted me at the door with, *"Just don't break anything."* Whenever I walked through the rooms I just prayed that I could remember and adhere to all her rules.

To further alienate me, Aunt Catherine would always escort my older sister to the back bedroom to spend time with her daughter Joann. She was bed ridden with cerebral palsy. My sister was allowed private moments with Joann before the rest of us could enter the room to greet her. We were only permitted a soft *"hello"* from the doorway.

I once asked my mother why my cousin Joann had to spend all of her time in bed. I wanted to know if she would ever get better and be able to walk like other children. My mother told me that when Aunt Catherine and Uncle Nick got married, they had a lot of money. The funds came from controlling interest in the Amrhein Bakery that had been established by his brother, Christopher, in 1888. This bakery survived the Depression and, in 1929, was moved to Clear Lake Avenue.

Suddenly, Aunt Catherine could afford a life filled with expensive clothes and luxurious travel. Aunt Catherine became obsessed with the way she looked. When Aunt Catherine got pregnant with Joann, she didn't want people to know that she was pregnant. Even as her body began to change and grow with the pregnancy, she would wear corsets that she would pull tighter and tighter to disguise her pregnancy. According to what my mother said, this restricted the growth of Joann, and she was not able to develop normally during the pregnancy. I still don't know if this is the medical reason for Joann's disability, but I certainly could imagine Aunt Catherine behaving in this manner.

The Sisters, Three have passed away as well as all of their siblings. My parents are dead as well. My siblings and I have grown into adulthood with children of our own. Otto Joseph, my paternal grandfather, died from head trauma from falling off of the back of a street car on his way home from a local tavern in Springfield, Illinois. The harsh imprint made by Otto Joseph can still be seen in our lives. He passed down his harsh and quarreling attitudes to our parents, William and Arlene.

As in childhood, our parents never seemed to have their needs met in life – they were two needy people who got married. They took their disappointments out on their children in many forms of physical and mental abuse. Within me is a fire that has been kindled against this pattern of neglect and abuse. Although the flames of success were greatly missing in my youth, they have blossomed into a blaze throughout my adulthood. It began with my search for my family history. First it whispered, then it talked, it slowly sang, and then finally yelled and screamed for me to find the grit that lit the fire that my people must have had to propel them into venturing towards this new world.

I like to imagine that my great-grandfather had a silent, conversation with his descendants while on that boat. He would have told us that he was bringing the family to a new, better life. Well, I have taken that bold thread made from the grit of my ancestors and used it to change things in myself for the better. I would like to think that my great-grandfather would approve of the manner in which I have used the flame that he carried to the "new country."

Somehow I wish that my ancestors would have found a way to soften their intensity. It is certainly important to be able to focus intensity when a person is trying to achieve a goal – either resettling into a foreign country or learning a new language. However, when parents are raising a family the children need to be valued and nutured as human beings. Parenting is a skill which hopefully blends these talents in a positive fashion.

Chapter 3

Arlene Freida Ada Ida Potata

One afternoon, when I was about eight years old, I asked: *"Mom, what is your middle name?"*

Her response was, *"Arlene Freida Ada Ida Potata."*

I laughed. It was unusual for my mother to show a sense of humor, and it came as a complete surprise to me. I expected her to say something like Mary, Sue, or Anna.

I pondered this interaction for a few days and decided that she must be telling me a joke. I asked again, *"Mom, what is your middle name?"*

Still, she continued to insist that Freida Ada Ida Potata was indeed her middle name. She responded quickly, *"What, you don't believe me?"*

I let her know that I didn't think that my grandmother, a quiet, kind, and intelligent lady, would name her child such a silly name. Finally, she told me that her middle name was Freida, and she thought the rest was cute to say.

This interaction, small as it may have been, happened to be my only real conversation with my mother in my memory. It was a rare moment where she revealed a sense of humor and shared a smile. It offered me a very small, yet telling, glimpse into a normally sad and angry woman.

My mother's demons were deeply imbedded within her soul long before I entered her life. They were probably planted there early in her childhood.[8] My mother's father was an intense, stoic farmer, also of Germanic descent.

---

[8] Wolvin, A. & Coakley, C. G. (1995) Listening (5th Ed.). McGraw-Hill.

Family history and my brief interactions with him revealed a guarded, strict person. My mother often stated that she was not her fathers' favorite, and she desperately had wanted to occupy that space. In fact, she told me that she had "acted out" a lot when she was growing up so that she would at least get her dad's attention. Since I could understand completely the feelings of an uncherished child, I believe that their father/daughter interaction was the seed that grew into my mothers' rage and discontent.

****

I'm five years old. I am enrolled in kindergarten at a private, Catholic school. It's a blustery, midwestern winter day. We're returning to class after recess. The Old wood and brick building offers warmth so we're all in a hurry to seek shelter in its toasty interior. I hustle in the door without wiping my wet shoes. After hanging my coat and hat up on a hook outside the classroom in the hallway, I run into the room. I want to get to the writing table first.

Slipping on a rug, I fall and hit the left side of my head on the sharp edge of the table. Everything goes foggy. The next thing I know, I am in the bathroom next to our classroom. I am standing beside the nun who was my teacher. We are in front of the sink. She is rinsing my head as blood flows down the drain. She keeps yelling at me to be still. I look at my favorite green sweater that I'm wearing and realize that it's also covered with blood. I don't know what happened, but I know that I am in trouble.

The nun keeps rinsing my head, and the blood just keeps dripping down the side of it. I watch the thin red lines seep and trickle down the inside the sink. I'm feeling woozy. I want to sit down. The nun just keeps yelling at me. Finally, after what seems like an hour, the nun tells me sit in a chair and hold a white cloth on the side of my head. *"Hold it there hard, and don't take it off!"* she said with concern and irritation.

I sit on a chair in the hallway and wait until she hands me my coat and instructs me to put it on. We walk together to the bus stop about two blocks away. What a strange experience it was–the nun and I walking down a street in the middle of the day. She waits with me until the city bus arrives.

"Don't talk to anyone on the bus," she tells me as I get aboard.

The husky man sitting behind the steering wheel suspiciously looks me in the eye and says, *"Get in the back, and don't mess around. I don't want any trouble."*

I do as instructed. After all, I hope to have some small chance of getting into heaven, someday.

It takes about an hour to travel to my usual bus stop. Before I get off, I open my coat. When the bus driver sees my sweater, he sucks in a deep breath, lowers his head and his eyes squint. I look down and realize that my favorite green sweater is now crusted with brownish, red blood. I feel woozy again. I step off of the bus, walk about three blocks, and lumber through the back door of our house.

My mom doesn't expect me to show up at home in the middle of the morning. *"Why are you here? How did you get home? What kind of trouble are you into now?"* She strongly grips my arm as she asks a barrage of questions filled with irritation and surprise. The blood stained bandage enveloping my head is ignored. I can't think, but I desperately want to avoid the sting of the back of her hand. I fling open my coat and show her my now ruined sweater. She stares at me with a confused look on her face. Slumping my head and shoulders, I quickly tell her the story of hitting my head at school, the nun rinsing of my head in the sink, and the frightening bus ride home. When I finish, we stand there looking desperately at each other. Slowly, she releases the grip on my arm.

I want her to give me a hug. I am confused, scared, and tired. To make my mental state even worse, I think that I have done something very, very wrong. She turns away from me without fulfilling my wish and heads toward the telephone. After phoning the neighbor for a ride, we drive to Dr. B.'s medical office a half-an-hour away.

As I sit in the waiting room, I am terrified about what was going to happen. I think that I am in trouble for ruining my good sweater. My mom never speaks to me while we sit, waiting.

When we enter the doctor's office, he examines me and has a brief conversation with my mother. Then we return home. By this point, I desperately want a hug. Still, I get none.

At home, my mom instructs me to put on my pajamas and go to bed. I throw my favorite green sweater in the trash. My mom informs me that I have a concussion, and I am to stay in bed for two days. Without explaining anything else, she picks up a basket of wet laundry and walks outside to hang it on the line.

I don't know what a concussion is. I decide that I had some kind of brain tumor, and it will take two days for me to die. I go to bed and wait. Over the next two days, questions fill my mind: *Who will make the funeral arrangements? Who will come?* I try to imagine what my casket will look like.

Throughout my ordeal, I was never offered or received a hug, a kind word, a soft touch, or a kiss on the forehead. A few days later, I returned to school still confused about everything that had happened.

****

This interaction with my mother was very typical. I learned early not to rely on her for comfort or reassurance.

This apathetic attitude was obvious one Saturday morning when my older sister, some friends, and I went ice-skating on the pond next to Harvard Park golf course. During the bitterly cold winters, we would split our time between ice skating and sledding down the snow-covered hill with doors from an old icebox or sturdy cardboard from large shipping boxes. After spending a few hours with a group of neighbor friends, we would head home cold, hungry, and tired.

On this particular Saturday, I noticed that a sign had been posted a short distance from our usual skating area. The sign read: *"Thin ice. Do not skate. Keep off."* The area had also been sectioned off with a large chain to make sure that people did not wander into the area by mistake.

Children have interesting minds. In my case, instead of accepting the warning, I began to wonder if the ice was really thin or if it were just being saved for adults to use later in the day. I decided to cross over the line. This was something that I have done throughout my life–crossing over into the danger zones–especially in situations where danger signs had been clearly posted.

I skated for a few minutes on the thin ice. When nothing happened, I began to feel confident with my theory. As soon as the other kids noticed that I had crossed the line, they started yelling for me to come back. I did not listen. Instead, I yelled at them to come and skate on the clean ice. They all refused, pointing out the sign and the rope.

After several minutes of skating alone, I got bored and decided to leave the roped off area to join the group. It was then that I heard a faint cracking sound. Fear raised my heartbeat, and I instinctively skated faster. The cracking sound grew louder - as if the sound wanted to catch me. Suddenly, I was sucked into the cold, dark water.

After feeling emotionally isolated my entire life, I was finally physically isolated from everything and everyone. When I reached the muddy goo at the bottom of the pond, I floated back to the surface. Once near the top, though, I could only see frozen ice above my head. I couldn't find the ice hole through which I had fallen.

Many leaves and twigs had frozen in the ice with bits of dirt and pieces of small rocks held captive within the flat, crystalized slab. I looked upward, and the sparkling beauty of the debris captured my total attention. I was quickly lured into a sense of false security by their hypnotic beauty. As my water logged body slowly drifted toward them, I struggled to lift my hands to touch them.

Again, I realized with a fleeting moment of terror that I couldn't find the jagged edges of the hole where I had fallen through. However, that fact was suddenly not important. It was restful just to stay in the welcoming, wet home and to touch and caress the frozen jewels.

I felt my body descending back down to the bottom of the murky pond again. My many layers of clothing were thoroughly soaked and heavy. They pulled me toward the welcoming mud.

I looked up at the kaleidoscope of shapes and colors. It was beautiful and inviting. My thoughts returned to my need. My body ascended, almost without effort on my part, toward the crystallized slab. I reached my hands upward but the entry hole eluded me.

My body descended again down toward the welcoming bog. The thick clothing formed a heavy cocoon providing me with the comfort I never had received or experienced at home. It felt as if I were in the one place on earth where I was truly welcomed and safe. My heart welcomed me to stay—the depths accepted me as I was. Still, there was a part of me that screamed to live. I forced my reluctant body toward the crystallized slab. Finally, I found the rough edges of the hole. My arms and head broke the surface while the intruding light of the sun stung my eyes. I was disappointed and relieved at the same time.

I squinted and spotted several of the kids I had been skating with standing in the distance. The minute figures were looking in my direction, yelling, and frantically waving their arms like miniature vibrating stick men. However, I couldn't hear what they were saying.

I tried to heave my soaked body out of the icy cavern, but it wouldn't release its hold. In fact, the toothed edges kept breaking off, making the cavern bigger with each attempt. I realized that even though I had my head above water, I still wasn't free from the icy grip of death. A dreaded thought overwhelmed me: My skating partners couldn't help me. If they tried to skate onto the roped-off ice area, they also would meet the same dire fate. A chill traveled down my spine. They could see me but they couldn't rescue me. They would watch me die.

As I looked at them in the distance I noticed that they were sliding a long pole toward me across the ice. My older sister was pushing it toward me in an attempt to help while the other kids lay flat on the thicker ice I watched in slow motion as the pole advanced across the icy tundra.

Blindly, I groped at the lifeline. I could only guess when my frozen hands made contact. My numb fingers instinctively held on for dear life. I knew this was my last chance. I felt a jarring tug once and then again. This time the heartless, arctic water released its clench.

I knew that my survival depended on maintaining my grip. I was pulled, much like a beached whale, across the ice. I was transported from the dangerous roped-off area to the safe skating area. Slowly, I became aware of the voices and screams of my frantic skating buddies.

The next challenge was to get home so I could get dry and stay warm since there was no way to call our parents. We were at a public park and this was a time before electronic cell phones or computers. There were no public phones. None of us had cars or even bicycles. The only mode of transportation available was a small, one-person sled which we planned on using after we were done skating. We had made arrangements for a parent to pick us up but that would be much later in the day.

My body was soaked and frozen. My hands and feet wouldn't work. I was crying because I was so scared. I wanted a hug. I needed to be warm, but I couldn't think of any solutions. My sister was yelling. In fact, everyone in the group was yelling at me!

They finally decided to put me on the sled while my sister pulled me home. It was about a half-mile to the edge of the park and, from there, it was only half a block to our home. I fell onto the sled. My sisters' yelling and cussing continued as we set off but was mixed with other colorful words. She yelled and cussed and I cried all the way home.

When we finally arrived at home, I struggled to get off of the sled but couldn't. The cold weather and my wet clothes had meshed into a solid block of ice. I tried to rock my body back and forth but there were no signs of the ice breaking. My sister walked a short distance from the sled, turned and then ran back toward me at full speed. She turned sideways, crunched-up her body, and plowed into my shoulder. A loud cracking sound rang out and the ice released its binding grip. I fell sideways off the sled into the snow, finally able to lift my arms and unfurl my legs.

Trudging around to the back door of the house, I stumbled through the kitchen door. I was sobbing, shivering, soaking wet, and caked with ice. The snot from my nose and the tears from my eyes had frozen in small clusters on my beat red, frostbitten face.

My mom was standing next to the kitchen counter. Our eyes met, and for one brief, desperate moment I thought that this finally might be the one point in time when my mother would acknowledge that I did have a warm, meaningful place in her heart. Instead, she quickly released the visual hold and returned to her baking task. At that moment, I knew I would forever have to be my own comforter.

My sister struggled to tell the story, but my mother waved her away, bringing up the back of her flour-covered hand over her head. Without emotion or concern, she yelled at me for wearing my ice skates in the kitchen and for getting the kitchen floor wet.

I so very desperately wanted a hug, a warm blanket, and a kiss. I wanted my mother to care that I had just cheated death. Mom offered no such support. Sternly, she instructed me to change my clothes. Thankfully, I was allowed to set in front of the heat register in the kitchen for the next couple of days so that I could warm up.

It took two days for the throbbing pain in my extremities to subside. I watched as the color of my hands and feet slowly transformed from a deep purple, to white, to red and finally rosy pink. My aunt told me that my hands and feet would probably hurt for the rest of my life when the weather temperature turned cold because I had frostbite. She was correct.

****

There are other issues which still shiver my soul. I still don't fully understand why my mother beat me, but beat me she did. She would beat my sisters and brother, as well. Whenever we did something that she did not like, she would grab the closest thing she could find and best us until she was exhausted. She would often use a kitchen broom, the cord from an iron, a stick, or a shoe. She liked to use anything that was handy.

Her favorite whipping tool was a tree branch from the weeping willow in our back yard. When she decided that we had done something particularly bad, she would instruct us to go outside to the willow tree and cut a long, branch from it. If she was not satisfied - meaning that if it was not thick enough or if it did not have enough sway to it when she slashed it through the air over her head - she would have us go out to get another branch. She would keep sending us back for another one until she was satisfied.

Once the preferred weapon was in hand, she would take a deep breath and transform into a monster from some late night horror movie. Her outstretched arm would swing the branch downward until I felt the cutting sting on my buttock, back, or calf of my leg. It was never in the face where people could see the scar or bruise or cut.

Her voice bellowed out in a low pitched, raspy tone as she struck my flesh, *"Don't cry, or I'll beat you harder. Just stand still and take it."* It was important to my mother that as she hit me I didn't acknowledge the damage to my skin, the cuts into my tender, young flesh, despite the intense pain. It was as if she were trying to release a powerful, horrible force from her own childhood while denying that she was actually destroying the relationship she could have with her own child.

The beatings would continue until my skin was broken and my mother could see the damage that she had done. At that point, it seemed as if the force of her attack intensified until bright red blood was visible. These final strikes were most intense. Although they cut the tissue the deepest, I knew that the beating was almost over. The unknown mission of my mother's tortured mind had been accomplished. The beating was to me an outward

29

sign of the demon within her. My mothers' arms were tired. My back and legs were covered with bruises and cuts that would soon turn to scars.

My mother continued beating me like this until I reached the age of about fourteen. Why did she quit? I guess that she was too busy beating my younger brother and sisters to waste her energy on me. During the beatings, I came to believe that she was trying to hit me hard enough to release the demon from within her.

****

I was not the sole object of my mother's fury. Similar abusive scenes were repeated on my siblings. One particular incident will be forever seared into my mind. I was a freshman in high school. It was about eight o'clock at night, and I was doing homework in my bedroom. My mom was putting my little sister, M., to bed. Her crib was in my mom's bedroom. At the tender age of 10 months, my mom had decided that my sister was old enough to go to sleep in her crib without a nighttime bottle.

Until this dreadful night, my baby sister had always gone to bed with a bottle. As she lay in her crib, she began to cry for her bottle. My mom returned to the bedroom and slapped my sister in the face with the full force of her open hand.

"You're not getting a bottle! Now shut up, and go to sleep!" my mother screamed at her. Of course, my little sister didn't understand, so she kept crying. My mother repeatedly came into the bedroom, slapped my sister, and yelled at her to shut up and go to sleep. When I could endure it no more, I tentatively moved into my mom's bedroom to help my sister.

I saw M. standing in the crib. Her little fingers were covered with slobber, tears, and thin streams of blood as she gripped the bars. Every fiber of my being told me that I had to muster all of my courage to help my sister. I couldn't let her endure this trauma I had endured; she was so very little.

I walked up to the crib and stood between my mother and my little sister. *"Mom, quit. You are going to kill her,"* I said this as I muster my courage.

My mom slowly tilted her head toward me. Her body was hunched over like an old oak tree. She looked me straight in the eye with two pools of black hatred and burning evil. *"Get out of the way, or I will start beating on you,"* the words flying viciously from her mouth.

I knew that was exactly what she would do. I had tried to interrupt my mothers' hate rages on my siblings before and had always come out beaten and bruised. I shook with fear as the sickening, yellow, barfing feeling of cowardice vibrated throughout my body. My bravery instantly evaporated. I lowered my head and stepped aside.

Her hand swung down, and she slapped my little sisters' face again. The yell, which echoed up from M.'s tender little mouth, pierced through my body like shards of broken glass, gashing through tender, supple skin. Blood gushed willingly from my little sisters' swollen cheek. Her tiny, fragile fingers released their fading grip from the crib rail. M.'s body crumbled to the mattress, and she huddled in a shaking, whimpering ball of fear and pain.

I cadly turned away and left the room knowing that if I attempted to comfort my sister at that moment, my mother surely would have beat me with raging force. I am ashamed, to this day, that I didn't protect and comfort my little sister. Cowardice haunts me – even the memory ignites a queasy response. M., I am so very, very sorry!

The next morning, I dressed for school. M was sitting in her highchair in the kitchen when I entered the room. I couldn't look at her. I ever so gently kissed her soft, tender head.

M. never cried for her nighttime bottle again. When mom put her in her crib at night she would very, very quietly lie down and turn her face away. She had learned what we, the rest of us, already knew. There would be no good night kiss, no hug, no bedtime story, and certainly no bedtime bottle.

Many years later, while talking to M. on the phone, I discussed this incident with her. She did not remember it but shared other multiple abusive incidents which she did remember.

As an adult, I believe discipline should be used by parents to teach children valuable lessons for life. However, punishment should be used by society for citizens who refuse to follow rules in order to keep society safe. In our house, the lines were blurred. After periods of intense punishment, we were left confused about why they had occurred. Rules usually changed without warning.

Although mom dished out stern punishment for unknown infractions, she was careful never to do it in front of others – neighbors or extended family members. There was never discipline that taught us how to be better, always punishment. As an adult, I can only conclude that we were punished for making her life less than ideal, less than what she had expected, and less that what my father promised.

Whatever demons lurked inside my mother, they prevented her from expressing nurturing moments toward her children. My mother chose not to confront those demons and that refusal has caused so many family members intense pain. She missed the warm, snugly moments of kissing and hugging with her children. My mom never experienced a mothers' special, loving time when she cuddles with her child who was just waking up from a restful nights' sleep. She never felt the sweet, warmth of the child as it lingered in the covers. She missed the unconditional love that a small child gives to someone they truly care for and missed the child's generously bestowed loving smile. I was never sure, but I always suspected that her own father must have treated her similarly as a child. Perhaps my mother was always searching for that illusive paternal love.

****

My mother did everything with intensity. One of her more degrading habits was to sing *"silly, degrading Joyce songs"* that she had invented. One such little tune was:

Inside. Outside. Backwards. Joyce.

Another little tune was:

Joycie Poycie puddin and pie – Kissed the boys and made them cry. When Joycie Poycie came out to play, All the boys would run away.

She would sing these songs over and over. She sang when I had trouble getting dressed in the morning, when my fingers wouldn't work well tying my shoes, or when I was trying on a new piece of clothing - often these were sung in public. Once the neighborhood kids knew them, they were repeated day-in and day-out just to irritate me.

Looking at my mother with child's eyes, I realized that if she beat me on a regular basis and tormented me with humiliating songs that she must have hated me. To be hated by my mother meant that I had no worth to the world - this was the lesson my mother taught me.

As an adult, I have only one happy moment in my memory: *"What is your middle name?"*- Freida Ada Ida Potata. I had only one smile from her to cherish.

Looking at the relationship with adult eyes, it is as if I never had a mother. I have had to comfort myself. I had to discover right from wrong for myself. I innately knew that I was a good person capable of forming a loving, caring, giving relationship with others. However, it has been and continues to be psychologically challenging. I prefer spending time by myself. I do not need to interact with others to feel complete. But after a long time alone, I do miss the smiling face of an innocent child, hearing the excited voice of an active teenager, or listening to the concerned voice of an educator trying to relate a scientific idea.

I am constantly discovering new avenues for expressing my attachments to other humans. Experiencing conversations with others on a daily basis is enjoyable. The neighbor, postman, or delivery van driver can offer a different perspective on current world events. This discussion can help form an opinion that broadens my worldview. These daily interactions keep my brain and body active and healthy. I also decided to enter the helping profession of nursing to assist me on that quest of forming attachments. It is self-fulfilling when you help others stay healthy.

The interactions between my mother and I strongly influenced my adult life. Hopefully, I have been a compassionate parent to my own children. I have learned that raising children encompasses love, guidance, and thoughtful discipline. It does not include abuse. It does not include physical violence—no matter how tired, irritated, or frustrated the parent happens to be. I had to break the cycle of violence that was inflicted on me as a child in order for me to effectively parent my own children into productive adults. Part of this process meant acknowledging the child abuse and its effects on me.

All young children desperately need to bond with at least one mature, functional adult. This bond assures the child of a loving place in the world. It encourages the child's self-worth. Unspoken messages of acceptance enable the child to develop self-identity. This base is an important framework for a productive, mature, functional adult. Once a child gets a firm stance on firm ground, then he or she is ready to face the world in a positive manner to deal with challenges that come his or her way.

Chapter 4
The Red-Headed Dutchman

Otto Joseph, Ludwig's youngest son, lived a long but dastardly life - dying September 1948 at the age of 77, one year before my birth. When I look at the wedding picture of my paternal grandparents, I see two placid-faced adults obviously uncomfortably dressed in their "Sunday-go-to-meeting" outfits. Their faces are almost stern looking—as though neither of them dare to betray any emotion. My grandfather, Otto, is seated in a stern, posed position with his gloved hands resting on his knees. My grandmother, Magdalena, is standing on his left side with her right hand lightly resting on his back, their bodies barely touching. She has a slight expression of anxiety on her face. Magdalena's sister, Sophie (Steiren) Raylots, is seated to Otto's right with her husband, Michael, standing behind her. The notation at the bottom of the picture indicates that it was taken at "Kessberger and Georg" studio in Springfield, Illinois, May 17, 1899.

My father, William Charles Gatschenberger, was born June 25, 1913 in Springfield, Illinois, the youngest of thirteen children. His father, Otto Joseph Gotschenberger, had been the youngest child of Ludwig and Maria (Lell) Gotschenberer. Ludwig Gotschenberger's passport indicates that his last name was spelled with an "o." The spelling changes after he arrived in the United States and the "o" is replaced with an "a": Gatschenberger."

From all accounts, my father grew up devoid of parental attention. His older half-sisters, Aunt Catherine, Aunt Mayme, and Aunt Sophie were his surrogate caregivers. When my father was born, my grandmother gave birth at home. He weighed ten pounds and was much larger than her pelvic area could accommodate. The complicated birth did a massive amount of internal tissue damage. She wasn't taken to a hospital for medical attention. As a result, she never recovered fully from the birth or regained her health. She was bedridden until her death a few years later.

My paternal grandfather was by all accounts a very stern taskmaster who showed little to no affection for his family. He would tether my young father and other siblings to a pole at night in the greenhouse to make sure none of his produce was stolen. I am sure that this had a very profound negative effect on my father. I can only imagine how it felt to have your father tie you to a pole at night in a dark, damp greenhouse leaving strict orders not to fall asleep or let anyone steal the tomatoes and onions? I am sure that it gave a clear message to all that the vegetables were more important than the child. Maybe this is why when my father became older he seemed to find solace working in the backyard garden for hours at a time to the state of exhaustion. Maybe all that chopping and hoeing was really him chopping and hoeing at his own father.

My father's education and rearing were provided by his three older sisters—his surrogate mothers. My grandfather was not affectionate, attentive, nor monogamous. He had many girlfriends during his marriage and often brought them home and introduced them to his children. Aunt Mayme told me that when my father was entering his teenage years and before he went into the army, she, Aunt Catherine, and Aunt Sophie moved out of the house into an apartment in town to escape my grandfather's physical abuse and sexual exploits.

My mother told me the story of her first meeting with my paternal grandfather. After repeatedly knocking at the front door of my grandfather's house, my parents entered and called out his name, but he didn't answer. They searched and followed the sounds of moans and groans until they found him in the bedroom in a sexual encounter with his girlfriend. My grandfather, according to my mother, didn't seem to be disturbed by the incident and without moving from the bed unceremoniously introduced his girlfriend to my mother. He made no excuse for his situation and did not attempt to cover his half-nude body or remove himself from his amorous position.

Aunt Mayme told me the first story I ever heard about my father's youth. Apparently, *"He spent his teen years turning over outhouses just to see the mess that it would make."*

He went before the local magistrate for destroying local outhouses. The neighbors were ready to testify, *"I'm sure that he was the boy who turned over my outhouse, judge, because I would know that red-headed Dutchman anywhere."* Since my father sported a full head of thick, flaming red hair, there was no way for him to deny anything!

As a child, I remember hearing stories from my aunts concerning the way he ran wild through the neighborhood and was in trouble on most days. The local magistrate finally gave my aunts a choice: jail or the army. They chose the army for him. He was assigned as a combat engineer in a special bomb squad troop.

My mother had moved from Nebraska to California, and was working as a beautician in her older sister's salon. My father was introduced to her through a mutual friend during his enlistment in San Diego. My mother became pregnant with my older sister during their courtship. The only acceptable societal solution for this situation was marriage. As soon as my father was released from the army after the Second World War, they were married in Galesburg, Illinois. (He was released from military service in Illinois since he had enlisted in Illinois.) They then moved to Springfield to build a home and raise their family.

In order to understand my father, I searched through his childhood and struggled to understand situations under which he was raised. He was always a very stern and angry man who seemed to get very little joy from life. Like my mother, my father never offered affection or emotional attachment to me as a child. I desperately needed a relationship with my father and always found it lacking. I grew up never experiencing the security of a loving family bond. I always questioned why he couldn't love me. I found a partial answer when I reviewed his childhood.

His formative years were devoid of nurturing, cuddling, encouragement, and parental concern. He grew up wild and unaccountable. In my mind, this information helped to explain, but in no way excuses, the style of parenting he used with my siblings and me. My father was always emotionally unavailable not only to me but all my siblings. I can't honestly remember one incident in my life when my father touched me, kissed me, hugged me, or said a kind word to me.

****

Like many children, I was curious about how I had received my name - I decided to ask my mother. I wanted to understand the process my parents went through to ensure that I had just the right name. I listened very intently to her response. She said that while she was still in the hospital, a few family members were visiting. They all had suggestions for names prior to my birth but no one could decide on one specific choice. My father told her that he wanted a son and was very firm about the name of "Jimmy or James." He would not even entertain a girl's name.

Everyone in the room wrote their name choice on a piece of paper, folded it, and placed it in a hat. My dad picked out a piece of paper on which was written "Joyce." *"I don't want a girl I want a boy,"* he said. He took the paper, wadded it up, threw it on the floor, and left the room.

I learned later in life that my younger cousin, who was born a few weeks later, was named "James." My father made it clear throughout my life by his words and actions that he was very disappointed that I was not a boy.

****

I remember my dad coming home each day from the post office where he worked as a route letter carrier. The opening of the front door would trigger the routine. It began with his demeaning voice, yelling about every bad thing we, the kids, had done – we left the door open; didn't turn the light off; hadn't finished our chores. Then, he would change from his work clothes into his yard clothes and work in the backyard garden until suppertime.

My mother would spend most of her day cooking supper from scratch. It was as if she expressed herself through her cooking. Every night, without fail, my father would complain about the food she had made for the evening meal—the meat wasn't cooked right; the beans tasted awful. Heaven forbid if the supper meal was not on the table exactly at 5:00 p.m.

Repeatedly, my mother would stand at the kitchen counter with her apron on, covered in flour from making dough for biscuits or bread. Even though she always baked all day, she did not always have supper finished in time. When my father walked in the door from work and found out that supper was going to be late, he would ball-up his right hand and punch my mother in the lower back. I would hear her let out a gasp of air, her knees would bend and buckle as she held onto the edge of the kitchen counter top for support. Not a word was spoken. Not a cry was let out. My father would turn and leave the kitchen. My mother would hurriedly continue her meal preparations.

My father's disagreeable manner would continue throughout the mealtime. After supper, I would watch my father as he would sit in *his* chair in *his* living room and drink *his* beer. He would finish the first glass, and his mood shifted to happiness. He would talk out loud as if he were conversing with an imaginary friend sitting next to him. He wouldn't stop there, though. As my dad drank the second and third glasses of beer, he would become quiet. By the fourth and fifth glasses, an alcoholic stupor would occur. He would sit still in the chair with his eyes closed as if he was living in the imaginary world of his mind. There was no pain. There was no obligation. There was no schedule to maintain. Somewhere around the sixth to eighth glasses, I would recognize the stage I later called the *"click."* I knew when my dad reached this point–when he felt the *click*–he would quit drinking for the night and somehow stagger down the hallway to bed. As a child, I simply needed to wait for the *click*, and then I knew that I could relax.

****

I am ten years old. It is a bitterly cold, mid-westerly, winter day. I stay after school to rehearse for an upcoming Christmas play at Sacred Heart Church, located next to the school. My dad is going to pick me up after the rehearsal at 4:00 p.m. The practice ends, and one-by-one the other children leave. Vehicles come. Children gladly jump into the open car doors with their warm interiors and welcoming parents. The nuns, who had played the organ and other musical instruments, leave the church and walk across the street to their convent house for the evening. The parish volunteers, who clean the altar and replace the flowers, leave the church, lock the doors, are greeted by their husbands, and are whisked away in cars to their homes. I continue to wait… and wait… and wait…

It was getting darker and colder. My dad had not arrived, and he had not sent anyone to pick me up or let me know that he would be late. This was in a period before people had access to cell phones or computers. I had no way of knowing what to expect. I had nowhere to go and no way to call someone. I guessed that it was about 6:00 p.m. It was pitch dark and bitterly cold. The church was miles from my house. If I walked home, I would have been frozen before I got there.

I had tried all of the tricks I knew to keep warm. I stomped my feet, danced around, and sang the new Christmas song I had just learned. I blew my warm breath into my freezing hands. Nothing seemed to work. My entire body felt like a frozen icicle. I stomped around the barren tree in front of the church so many times that the snow was beaten into brown, muddy goo.

By this time, my feet were frozen into numbness. I had been crying, and the tears had frozen on my cheeks. I was scared that my dad would never come. I had heard stories of parents abandoning their children and began to believe that this might be one of those situations. People would read about it the next morning in the newspaper.

I was getting desperate. I was shaking uncontrollably, and I wasn't sure if it was from the cold or from the fear of dying alone. It was very dark, and I was so very cold. I started to walk down the street toward my house but became scared that I would freeze to death alone in the darkness. I turned around and ran back to the church. I was terrified that the janitor who came to the church in the morning to unlock the door would find my frozen body in the brown goo around the tree.

I knew that the nuns lived close to the church in their convent house. However, I, as a good Catholic girl, knew I could not disturb them after school hours. It was better to freeze to death alone in the dark. I didn't want to go to hell. I wanted to have at least a slim chance of making it to heaven. I hoped that if the nuns found my body in the morning on their way to mass, they would give me a Catholic burial.

I slumped down next to the barren tree, confident that it was my only friend. I wedged one of my schoolbooks under my bottom to place a protective barrier between my vulnerable body and the frozen ground. I folded my arms around my contracted legs, lowered my head, and closed my eyes. I was exhausted. I needed to rest.

A few minutes can seem like an eternity for a scared, cold, forgotten child. I don't know how long I sat under the tree, but it seemed like hours. Eventually, I thought I could hear the faint sound of a nearing car. Slowly it grew louder and pulled up to the curb by the church where it stopped. The car was about half a block from where I had found solace next to the tree.

I struggled to move, but most of my clothing had frozen. By twisting my head, I could see my father's silhouette in the driver's seat. I wanted to jump up, run to him, throw my arms around him, and say, *"Thank you for rescuing me from the frozen tundra!"* My body wouldn't move. My voice also failed me. It was as if the tree wouldn't release me.

With all my might, I lunged forward. My frozen body fell to the side of the tree and landed in the snow. My dad rolled down his window.

"Get up! Let's go," he said gruffly. I tried to release myself but my body wouldn't move. I was as if my bones were cemented in a fetal position. I prodded and pushed but my arms and legs would not unfold.

"I don't have all day. Get over here!" I tried again to stand. After great effort and determination, my limbs unfurled. I was able to stand on my numb, frozen feet. After I wobbled to the car, I opened the back door and slumped into the back seat. I knew it was useless to ask any questions or to tell my dad that I was scared and cold. He wasn't concerned.

"I had to take your sister to the store to get something for school. I took her home and remembered that I forgot you. I had to come back." He turned in the seat toward my general direction as he told me, but never made eye contact. I listened, numbly, as the cold words crashed into my frozen ears. We said nothing to each other on the way home. The silence was expected however, I thought that somehow this time there may be some sign of affection.

When we got home I would have loved to tell my story to curious and concerned family members. But, I knew not to expect any interest or comfort. In reality, I simply walked through the door, went to my bedroom, and fell asleep, fully clothed, on my bed. There were no kisses, no hugs, and certainly no warmed blankets.

****

When my mother designed our house and my father built it, it was completed in stages. The basement was built first. That meant that our family lived in it for a few years before the upstairs was completed. My older sister and I were small children when the upper level of the house was finally built. My parents decided not to install a shower in the bathroom upstairs since there was a full bath with a shower on the ground floor.

However, they did install a bathtub upstairs with a cabinet next to it for storing extra toiletries, (soap, tooth powder, wash cloths, towels). The bottom shelf of this cabinet was removable for easy access to all the plumbing between the upstairs and ground bathrooms. There were multiple spaces between the convoluted plumbing pipes so that a person could see through the bottom of the upstairs bath cabinet into the shower of the downstairs bathroom.

Everyone in the house knew about this removable shelf between the bathrooms. When I entered my teen years I preferred to take a shower instead of a bath–it just felt more comfortable. After running the water a few minutes, I would hum my favorite tune, not loudly, just at a low level the way that someone does when they are feeling safe and relaxed.

Then I would hear a *thump*. The sound was familiar, but I couldn't quite identify the source. I completed my shower, dressed, and went upstairs. After walking upstairs to the kitchen, I asked mom if she ever heard unusual noises coming from outside when the shower downstairs was being used, and she said no. I dismissed the sound.

This strange situation occurred periodically over the next few years. Finally, I got so frustrated that I decided that there must be something wrong with the plumbing system. I went down stairs and turned the water on. Then I went back upstairs to the bathroom. After some investigation, I pinpointed that it was indeed coming from inside the house, but I still couldn't pinpoint the exact spot. I proceeded to knock on the walls, stomp on the floor, and open and close the medicine cabinet door. Then I began throwing brushes and combs on the floor and bouncing bars of soap off of the bathtub. Nothing seemed to make the same sound. I could hear the water running in the downstairs shower stall bathrooms. I knew it was still going.

Then it came to me! I glared at the cabinet next to the bathtub. Reluctantly, I grabbed onto the handle I stared at the bottom wooden shelf of the cabinet – a very, very long time. I didn't want to pick it up, but still I lifted the edge of the wooden shelf. I was even more reluctant to drop it down. I so dreaded the sound it would make. For several moments, I just held it, but finally, I let go. I recognized the sickening sound - immediately. This *thump* was THE THUMP, which I had been hearing so often while taking a shower downstairs. Someone in my family was watching me while I was taking a shower!

Years later I told this story to one of my younger sisters. She replied that she had the same experience. I think that until that moment each of us believed that we were the only sexually violated child. Child sexual abuse comes in many forms. A queasy feeling still fills my stomach when I think that a member of my own family had voyeuristic tendencies. I immediately suspected my father.

I wonder also if my mother knew of this voyeurism. A more detestable thought is that she knew what was happening and chose to ignore the issue! I have no words to describe my sense of hurt and disappointment.

****

There was always an intense, emotional, dark cloud that hung over our family. My father wasn't available either physically or emotionally to lift that cloud for his family. When I looked at him then through my fearful child's eyes, I didn't understand him. When I remember him now through my adult's eyes, my memories evoke anger. I mourn for the relationship we didn't have.

As a child, it was as if my father never acknowledged that I was alive. I needed to be told by a strong, nurturing, male figure in my life that I was lovable, pretty, and worth something. I needed to know that I was protected. Instead, all of my early childhood experiences taught me that my father was not, and would never be, that person.

I entered the adult world without an appropriate skill set for approaching social situations and solving problems. Still, I believed that I was as competent as my peers. When I was finally able to judge my skill set, I found my feelings of self- worth, the manner in which I related to men, and my interactions with other people were lacking. I realized that I was going to have to love myself, and I was going to have to protect myself.

A couple of years before my father's death, I went to visit my father in the Veteran's Care Home. By this time, he was suffering from early Alzheimer's disease. I wanted the meeting to be cathartic for me, but from the beginning, my father did not want to interact. I tried to draw him out—to get a response. I wanted so desperately to have him acknowledge me and apologize for the strife he had caused throughout my childhood. However, it was not to be.

Instead of being purified, I left with more frustration and anger than I had when I entered his room. I understood at that point that visiting him in what was to be the last stages of his life would not take away the burden he had forced me to carry. I decided it was best to not return. I realized that he was never going to have to atone for the misery and pain he had inflicted upon my siblings and myself. It is important for me to view my father in this manner at this point in his life and I finally understood that resolving my feelings concerning my childhood was my issue and not my fathers'. My father would never atone for his paternal crimes.

Chapter 5
"IT"

It sneaks and snakes through the crevices of my bones.
It swirls through my blood pumping heart.
It invades my thoughts and distracts my thinking.
It steals my private moments with the precision of a jewel thief.
It holds hostage and invalidates my most precious memories.
It invents unreasonable goals.
It betrays, distorts, and holds hostage my happy dreams.
It trudges through my hopes and wishes like a horde of savage warriors.
Its' rancid breath soils my relationships.
It coats my skin with a layer of silicone that clouds my current reality.
It eliminates, with a surgeons' precision, my full potential.
It discredits my educational achievements with lightning verbosity.
It is the baggage I carried into adulthood.
It, my bits and pieces of memories, is my fat childhood.

I was always fat - a fat baby of a fat mother. I have fat memories - reminiscing over fat pictures. I didn't realize that being fat would determine my place in life, my position in business, my social status, my admittance to higher education, and my "seat on the bus", but it did and it does. It is socially acceptable for a fat child to be the target of bullying. People in society, especially children, see the fat child as someone who has no worth. It is permissible to call the fat child names, spit on the fat child, and exclude him or her from athletic events because the fat child is not seen as an equal in the great sea of humanity. Being fat means being less–less deserving, less accepted, less worthy, less beautiful, and less lovable.

Memories of riding the city bus to school each day as a "less" person are vivid. The cruelty began when I would walk out the yard through the back gate and travel down the alley for a few blocks to catch the city bus. When meeting someone walking in the opposite direction along the path, whether an adult or child, my senses would heighten. I felt their condescending attitude toward me. The adults, who had acquired some level of civility, would simply avert their eyes, avoiding contact with mine and passing by me as though I were invisible. I saw them greet others on the street, smile at the children, and say, *"Hello."* The children, on the other hand, who had not yet been molded into polite society, would shout out disparaging remarks: *"Fatty, Fatty two-by-four can't through the kitchen door,"* or *"Lock up your ice box; tubby is coming."*

It seemed as if it were okay for these assaults to occur, for these knives of social insult to be slung at me. In my mind, I was a freak in a beautiful world. I was upsetting the visually beautiful picture and, therefore, deserved to be a target. In a way, I decided it must be my fault that I was being attacked. After all, the children were forgiven and their attacks were ignored, sanctioned by the adults. If anything, the adults simply urged their children to quicken their steps as they passed. Often, I didn't even know these mockers.

This scene continued when I boarded the bus. The driver looked at me with disgust if I fumbled with my bus fare or dropped one of my books. In my nervous state, I would have to bend down to pick up the dimes and usually end up also dropping my lunch bag. I then would have to bend over and pick up the lunch bag. *"Don't be so slow. I have a schedule to keep,"* he would bark.

I had learned at an early age that only the pretty people get to sit up front. They sit there so that they can be seen by the public and feel good about themselves. Pretty people are slim, walk evenly, and carry themselves upright with an air of confidence. They make eye contact and shake hands with a smile.

Everyone has an "It"–their own bits and pieces of memories from their childhood that coalesce to form their past. My personal *It*, which is the memory of my fat childhood was not destined to congeal and create a positive, strong, motivated adult. I had to eviscerate the entrails of my childhood. My first step was to remember the memories. I realized that they would always be part of me and so I needed to make them work for me instead of letting them, *"the It"*, entertain their power.

I physically matured, emotionally trudged through the quagmire associated with my fat memories, examined them, and did my best to filter out the negative feelings and impressions attached to this baggage. I struggle each day with *"It."* As an adult, I try to focus on the facts I know: I am a strong, educated, healthy adult filled with inner beauty. My adult-self is capable of dealing with the everyday challenges and trials that other people face each day.

Despite my mindset, I am not naïve enough to believe that I can avoid every situation of social aggravation. However, no longer am I vulnerable to attack. I listen less frequently to that softly whispering indecisive voice. I have realized that getting rid of the negative memories attached to *"It"* is a lifelong process.

****

Although I have worked hard to filter bad memories from my childhood, the scars of the memories remain, impossible to erase. My parents did nothing to reassure me that I was loved. If anything, their actions, such as forgetting about me while taking my sister to get things she needed, reinforced my view. An article published in Web MD (Nov./Dec/ 2014) relates that a UCLA study published in JAMA showed that over 50% of girls across the United States who had been told that they had a weight problem by the age of 10 (whether they did or not) were clinically obese by the age of 19. The girls who were "fat–shamed" by their parents were more damaged. The article goes on to say that the age of 10 is a sensitive period for girls' development. Cognitive "black and white" self-esteem attitudes are taken very seriously. Parents should always try to focus on positive conversations because these attitudes "stick" into the adult years.[9]

---

[9]   Kennedy, L. P. (2014) Fat-shaming kids can lead to obesity and low-self esteem. Are you guilty of it? WebMD Nov./Dec. p27.

Conversely, my parents conceived my older sister before they were married. I learned this from my mother. A simple review of my parent's marriage date and my older sister's birth date confirmed the matter. This was the horror of all horrors in that period of history. My parents never talked of it. Despite this, everyone coddled her against that stigma surrounding her birth. Why couldn't I be coddled from the stigma of being overweight?

My older sister was guarded, nurtured, loved, and protected because she was an accident–an accident that made my parents get married. It saddled my dad with a family he really didn't want, a family he wasn't ready to raise, but a family for which he must take responsibility. This secret guided every facet of our family life. I was a young child and certainly did not feel like the chosen child. I decided that there must be something in our family history that made my parents treat me the way they did – neglecting my emotional needs. It was then that I began looking into the past for answers. I began listening to the stories I could pry from the Sisters, Three and my parents. To deal with the rejection I was feeling, I needed to justify it in some way.

Chapter 6

Joyce Discovering, Discovering Joyce

As a child, my mental outlook was bleak: if I were attacked by a thief, the robber would come out empty-handed. I am not sure when I began to question this perception, reinforced by the adult interactions I had, but I think I must have still been in grade school.

The Catholic Church that provided my education spared no effort when it came to hell, fire, and brimstone. I was instructed by nuns, priests, and my parents that I could not deviate from their teachings–verbal and non-verbal–or I would certainly perish. However, through their actions they had taught me that I was unworthy. I could not accept this, so I began to deviate from what they had taught. I wanted to test the forbidden ice. I wanted to find out for myself what the real limits were. This desire was a double-edged sword. On one hand, I was asserting myself, but on the other, I felt alienated and could not get help when I needed it.

****

Our second grade class was preparing for first communion. In the Catholic faith, you are required to learn a large number of questions and answers based on the King James Bible–the catechism. This religious doctrine contained knowledge designed to prepare children and religious converts to spiritually enter the church community. The questions and answers that were memorized related to basic truths of the Roman Catholic faith.

In my particular school setting, which was very German, this meant that each set must be memorized word for word. If, heaven forbid, someone substituted a word or phrase for the correct term, that person was designated an unfit Catholic and wasn't allowed to be part of the First Communion class.

I decided to challenge this theory. When reciting memorized verses to the nun in front of the class, I deliberately substituted my own words for the printed text. The nun immediately stopped me and corrected my recitation. She instructed me to recite the text as printed. I asked why I couldn't substitute another word that I thought was more appropriate.

"You will not be ready for your First Communion since you do not sufficiently know the required doctrine. You will be the only one in the class not permitted to make your First Communion. Your soul will be unclean. You will not go to heaven," was her arrogant litany.

Well, this of course seemed like a perfectly ridiculous explanation to me. I didn't think that God would cast me into hell simply because I substituted a few words in the catechism. However, as an insecure second grader, I needed to be part of things in order to feel safe and accepted. The verbal threat of being left out of the group was enough to get me back in line. Secretly, I suspected that she was lying to me, but I didn't want to test God.

I recited my text correctly after that encounter. However, when the parish priest came to check on the progress of the communion class, the nun told him that all the children knew their text except for me. She said I was not able to memorize all of the requirements.

Although she intimidated me back to the path, I would continue to question the status quo throughout my life. After this, though, I closely examined the situation and evaluated the risk to me before I questioned anything openly. I realized that if I tempered the questions, the outcome would be better for me.

****

It was in elementary school and we were learning long division. In those days, we used a blackboard in the front of the room to display our class work. During math class, students would be called up to write their math work on it. The nun in my class took special joy in using the blackboard for embarrassing the slower students in the class.

Long division had a very difficult and intricate pattern which offered a challenge for me to figure out. I finally realized, later in life, that I am much better learning the soft sciences, such as sociology and psychology. Math and biology proved much harder for me to master. When I was called up to the chalk board at the front of the classroom, it not only caused me great anxiety but embarrassment as well. There is no way I could hide my discomfort from the nun, the class, or myself.

Every week, the nun would call me to the board during math class. I would attempt to write numbers on the board knowing well that the computations were wrong. She would then verbally degrade me while the class members laughed at me. I would get frustrated, cry, and be unable to complete the task. The class would laugh louder. Finally, the nun would sternly instruct me to sit down. She never explained my errors to me. She only told me I needed to work harder on my math problems.

I could not learn math without someone else showing me. Still, no one wanted to figuratively walk across the bridge to get me, and I did not know how to ask for the help. Instead of privately working with me through the problems, the nun passed the torch to my mother. She called and told her that I would need more study time at home working on long division.

My mom was not a good teacher. She would write down long division problems each evening. Sitting next to me with a leather belt on the table, she would ask me about a problem. If I responded with the incorrect answer, she would pick up the belt, snap it in the air so that it made a quick cracking sound, ask me to stand up and then swiftly whip the back of my calves – always above the back of the knee. My legs always carried bruises and red marks.

"Don't cry, or I will just hit you harder! You will learn this, or I will keep beating you!" I would get so upset that I couldn't think. She approached the work as though I were embarrassing her with my ignorance. If, by sheer chance, I gave the correct answer to the problem, I was so upset that I had no idea how I figured out the result.

This continued nightly through most of the third and fourth grade until my mom could not find any new flesh on the back of my legs to hit with the belt. When I think about it, I believe that maybe she just got tired of hitting me. She never apologized, and I still don't like to complete math problems that require division.

✳✳✳✳✳✳✳✳✳✳✳✳✳

There was a generally understood rule in our class that we were not allowed to chew gum. During a memory lapse, I brought some candy and gum to school that were left over from a Trick-or-Treat function the night before.

We were in the middle of working on our writing assignment when my hand inadvertently went to my dress pocket. I knew it contained a particularly alluring piece of strawberry flavored bubble gum. I was involved in the assignment and absent-mindedly took the delicious bubble gum out of my pocket, unwrapped it, and began chewing it. Just as my saliva mixed with the juicy flavor of the gum, I heard the loud cracking snap of an all too familiar sound. The nun had picked up the large ferule and snapped it down furiously on her desk.

Everyone knew that this was the sound of real danger. All activity froze. Even breathing ceased. I knew I was in trouble. I could feel the burning stare of the warden on me. I furiously tried to remember what I had done. I couldn't think. I dared not even look up at her.

"Joyce, are you chewing gum?" The piercing command cut through the classroom silence like a heat-seeking missile. I immediately knew that this would be the day I would die. Time moved in slow motion. I understood that the nun was aware of the answer. Apparently, she needed me to confirm it in front of my classmates before inflicting her punishment – I knew that this gave her pleasure. My small *"yes"* stiffened her posture, tightened her jaw, and reduced her eyes to scorching slivers. I could hear the *pap, pap, pap* as the yardstick intermittently smacked the rough skin on the palm of her left hand.

"Come up here." The words hissed out of her clenched jaw. As I slowly walked to the front of the classroom, she picked up a wooden step stool from the corner. *"You will stay there all day,"* the nun sternly stated as she pointed to the top step. She had me place the chewed strawberry bubble gum in a ball on my nose. Then, she turned away and continued teaching the rest of the class. The thought of chewing gum lost all its prior appeal.

The bell rang for morning recess. The nun instructed me to get down from the stool and carry it with me outside to the playground. I did. I was then made to stand on the step stool in the center of the playground with the gum on my nose.

I stayed there throughout morning recess and had to bring the stool with me back to class. I asked my friend, Jean Anne, if she could sneak me a drink of water, but she refused. She didn't want to feel the wrath of the nun. I stood on the stool with the gum on my nose during the rest of the morning classes. I stood on it during lunchtime, afternoon classes, and afternoon recess.

When class was dismissed at the end of the day, the nun finally allowed me to step down from the stool and use the restroom before dismissing me. However, at that time, all I wanted to do was to go home. I had already soiled my clothes.

At home, I took the wet clothes and burned them in the trash barrel behind our house, trying to burn the shame I felt. However, that shame was not as easily destroyed as the clothes.

This experience did not teach me to not chew gum in school. Instead, I learned that nuns and most other persons in authority usually are cruel beyond reason. I also learned the difference between punishment and discipline. I learned that punishment did not help me become a better person – it only hurt me physically and emotionally.

****

My discovery of feminine cultural secrets occurred when I was a young naïve girl. It befell me quite by accident and occurred while performing a very mundane task. One of my regular household chores was to empty the household trash. This entailed going to every room and emptying the trash from the smaller trash cans into a larger plastic bag. This bag's contents would then be added to the larger can in the kitchen. All of the house refuge would then be taken out to the backyard burn barrel. Our particular burn barrel was located in the alley.

One evening, as I was hauling our trash to the burn barrel, I noted the previous nights' refuge had not totally burned. Therefore, I had to start the fire to first burn the leftover trash and then add small amounts of the new trash to it.

While handling this most disagreeable task, I emptied the remnants from the bathroom trash more slowly than normal. That's when I noted a large red stained bandage wrapped in toilet tissue. I unfolded the swaddled bundle and found a thick, oblong, soft pad approximately 2 inches wide and six inches long. It was saturated with blood. It was the type of bandage that a person would use to cover a large cut or gash on a large part of the body such as the stomach, back or thigh area.

I tried to remember if anyone in the family had suffered a cut or incision that would require such as bandage. I couldn't think of any one going through minor surgery or talking about falling and suffering a large cut on their thigh or back. I emptied more trash and noted more wrapped, soiled bandages. It was obvious that someone who lived in our house had suffered a horrible accident and needed intense medical attention. I began to wonder if it had happened when I was at school or at night when I was asleep. Either way, my parents didn't want me to know about the incident.

Deciding to locate the origin of the bandages, I made sure that I emptied the trash carefully the next evening. I designed a plan for the collection. First, I would collect the refuse from each bedroom, then the bathroom and then the larger bag in the kitchen. I would look at the contents of each can in secrecy. Then I could determine which person in the house had been injured seriously enough to need a large bandage.

Evening came, and I put my plan into action. The collection in the bedrooms offered no evidence. I hit pay dirt in the bathroom. That is where I found a new collection of used bandages. However, since everyone in the house used the main upstairs bathroom there were still six potential suspects. I decided that I would need an accomplice to help with my search.

Usually my older sister and I did not view situations in the same light. She always seemed to be focused on less intricate matters, but I needed help in this investigative matter. Besides, I would not include her on the entire plan. I would just ask her if she had noticed anyone in the house who had an injury that might need a large bandage.

I decided to approach her the next day after school. We were in our bedroom, changing from our school clothes into our outside clothes. While sitting on my bed and putting on my socks, I casually said "Hey, did you see anyone wearing a large bandage on their leg or back."

She looked at me as if I were being my usual pesky and stupid little sister self.

She didn't even turn around to answer me and continued to change her clothes. *"No, and don't ask such dumb questions,"* she said. For a moment, I decided that I might have to continue to search out the puzzle of the soiled bandages by myself. To my surprise she turned around, walked over to me, looked me suspiciously in the eye, squinted, and said *"have you been going through my stuff, again?"*

"No, I'm just trying to figure something out," trying to be non-chalant

"What?" she snapped. I knew that if I wanted her help, I was going to have to let her know what I had found in the trash. I also knew that she usually thought that what I did was not worthy of her attention. She was three years older, in her first year of high school, and sometimes knew big sister stuff even though she didn't like to share it with me. After all, I was mostly good for nothing but bugging her.

Without thinking I blurted out, *"Somebody in the house is hurt really bad and trying to hide it."*

"You're stupid," she said, turning away from me as she spoke. However, I was in it for all the marbles at that point, and I wasn't going to leave this subject alone. I started explaining the entire situation as if someone turned on a well-oiled release switch. I told her the whole story: from collecting the trash to unfolding the bandages while empting the cans into the burn barrel outside. When I finished, I took a deep breath, relaxed my shoulders, and stared at her blankly.

To my surprise, she listened to my tale. Unexpectedly, her face contorted and she moved toward me. I couldn't tell if she was going to share a coveted secret or hit me. I hadn't often seen this mood in my sister. She never liked to give up her secrets and didn't do it easily. Unexpectedly, she asked me to sit down on the bed and listen to her.

Each of us sat on our own beds, which were on adjoining corners of the room. She lowered her head and acted as if she were going to recite something sacred like the Lord's Prayer. The tone of her voice lowered while she started talking about babies and how they were born. I had no idea why she was talking about these things. After all, I had just shared a confidence about a family member who was injured.

Our house was not a safe, nurturing place where family could count on sharing feelings or get support when one was scared or confused. I certainly was confused to see my sister taking time out of her routine to talk with me and explain something to me. At the same time, I could not have cared less about babies at that point. I wanted to know about the used bandages in the trash.

She explained that babies grew in their mothers' stomachs for nine months and then came out. She said that in order for a mom to have a baby grow in her stomach, she needed to feed her baby. She was still talking in a weird tone and had her head bowed as though we were about to receive a blessing in a church.

I finally had enough of that goofy stuff. I yelled. *"If you aren't going to help me with the trash and the bandages, just shut up."*

"You are so stupid," she yelled, jumping off the bed. *"You don't know anything. You do stupid shit."*

"Well, fine." I said.

"Well, fine," she said. She got right in my face and yelled. *"Those aren't bandages stupid head. They are menstrual pads."*

"What?" I asked. *"What is that? What are you talking about?"*

"Just shut up and listen," she yelled. *"Mom and I use them when we have our monthly periods,"* she blurted out.

Now, my sister was using words that she knew I had never heard. She often did this when she wanted to feel superior or when she had a secret, and she didn't want to tell me. She would just dole it out in little bits and pieces. That way, she could torture me for days and days until I finally felt like just clobbering her. She was certainly acting like she was playing one of her stupid games. I didn't want to play, but I certainly did want her help in figuring out who in our house was using the big, dirty bandages.

I could not think of a snappy, cutting verbal comeback. I really wanted to punch her but knew that if I did she would stop talking and certainly wouldn't help me with the whole, dumb, confusing thing. I wished that I had never taken out the trash or seen the stupid bandages. I didn't like my older sister very much because we saw the world so differently. When I needed something from her, she made my life especially difficult. Well, this was one of those times. Again, she told me to shut up and just listen. She said that the bandages that I found in the trash were menstrual pads.

She said women used these to catch blood if they were not pregnant and didn't need to feed a baby.

The look on her face told the story. She looked as if she had betrayed a secret and punched me in the stomach all at the same time. My sister was not generally sympathetic to my concerns and causes and this, I'm sure, was virgin territory for her.

As I stared into her guilty eyes, a steamy feeling of disgust worked its way up from my toes. It worked its way right in to my mouth.

"Yuck, thaw, spit, yuck." The words refused to forms intelligent comments. I just let the sounds fly. Finally, the words themselves formed a sentence. My ears heard my mouth say, *"Do you mean that the dirty bandages weren't bandages? You mean that no one in the house…? Do you mean that I touch your used period pads? This whole thing is so gross."*

She looked at me with half a smile and half a frown. She knew that she had wounded me but shared a secret. I knew instinctively that she got pleasure from this form of betrayal. However, in this case she could not withdraw the insult. This was not an insignificant indiscretion—one which small children share about everyday items. She had pushed me over a threshold. She had destroyed my innocence and exposed me to a universal truth—a truth that was known by adults but secured from children. This was a truth that should have been released lovingly as part of a child's natural beauty. It should then be released as a rite of passage. It should not have been blurted out by a belligerent sibling in the bedroom during an irrelevant conversation. Truly this was an *arc* in the *Line of Listening* at this juncture of my life. My sister took joy in shattering my most sacred veil of naivety – I tumbled into the adult world.

Of course, I knew that she was lying. She did things like this just to get me upset. This time, I wasn't going to let her get away with the sting. I demanded that that she tell me the entire story if her tale about period pads were true. I knew that she couldn't think that fast and would refuse to continue with the farce.

Instead, she sat back down on the side of her bed. She began a long recitation about female menstrual cycles, babies, birth, and the whole disgusting cycle of things that happen to girls' bodies as they get older. She topped off the fantasy by relating that this period thing occurred every month. Because of that, I would be finding a lot more dirty bandages in trashcans. She added that I had better not be touching them because they had been worn by her and mom in the private parts of their bodies. She said that the reason that a girl's body shed the blood was because they did not need the fluid to nourish a baby.

Well, I thought that she made up the entire story. She got pleasure by grossing me out whenever she got the opportunity. I walked over to her and punched her, a good one, in the stomach. She hit me right back. I returned with a hard slap on the arm. Next thing I knew, we were down on the floor in our bedroom tearing and biting at each other. Whenever we got into these battles, we both wanted to really hurt each other. This time I had it in my mind to finally hurt her badly because she had really lied to me. I just hated it when people thought that I could not figure out things for myself. She thought that since she was older than I was that she knew so much more about life than I did. The fight ended in a draw.

I decided that the only way I could truly resolve the issue of the soiled bandages was to sort through the trash for the next couple of weeks. If I noted that the bandages were present on a regular schedule, then I would concede that my sister was correct. If the soiled dressings occurred every day for a week and then ended, I would know that it had been a bandage for a wound that had healed.

I volunteered to empty the trash into the burn barrel for the next few weeks. I sorted through the trash before it was burned—making sure to wear thick, rubber disposable gloves.

Sure enough the pads appeared on a schedule month after month. This routine was just as my sister had stated. I hated her for being right. I hated her for knowing a special secret that I hadn't known. I hated her for destroying my naïve childhood. I especially hated her because she took pleasure in watching me endure the pain of losing my innocence and floating into the abyss of young adulthood. She enjoyed seeing that I did not know what to do with the information. I was devastated. I learned about the birds and bees by sorting through the burn barrel in the alley behind our house. This experience definitely constitutes a strong, intense, enduring and dark **arc** along the *Lines of Listening* between sisters.

When it was time for me to inform my own children about the sexual facts of life, I began the instruction at their birth. I considered each part of the human body equal to every other part of the body. Therefore, explaining the function of each part was a basic process. The mouth is made for eating, the eye for seeing, the ear for hearing, the foot for balance and walking, and the vagina for reproduction and sexual pleasure. They are all natural parts with functions necessary for human survival. It was no great secret, and, therefore, I refused to make the information forbidden to either adult or child. My children grasped the concept effortlessly. There would be no need for trash picking in my home.

Chapter 7

The Brown Wooden Box

The cherished brown, wooden box positioned on my shelf has been my traveling companion for many years. Gazing at it inundates me with emotions. The wood's acquired patina reflects the many loving touches it has endured from numerous viewings as each memory is revived. The bronze coating on the wood is as smooth as a silent pond and the grain appears warm and inviting much like a lazy summer afternoon. Just the sight of the box beckons me to pause from my busy schedule and relax in the memories of it contains. These induce me to reminisce about some of the few happy reminders of my childhood. The prized box was a gift to me from my 14-year old brother, Chuck. He handmade the box in shop class at St. James Trade School. I treasure the gift because it contains all of the sacred cows of my life. It is beautifully crafted and reflects the sentiments we share for each other.

When I examine the brown wooden box, I get distracted and am flooded with childhood memories about Chuck. Mental pictures shoot through my brain, and I have to take time out reliving the distracting memories so that I can get on with reviewing the mementos in the box. Once the memories are reappraised, I can walk myself through the items and sacred cows in the box. Each time I feel exhausted, but fulfilled when I finish. I make a mental effort to release the bad memories and embrace the good thoughts of my life. This process helps me to feel stronger as I go through my day.

****

I was seven years old when my brother was born in 1956. He was the first son in our family of three sisters and would be big brother to yet another younger sister. My dad always bragged about having a son. Whenever we attended a large family function, such as a Christmas celebration or family reunion, my father would say, *"We'll keep having kids until I get a boy."* I remember thinking that even though my dad didn't seem to love any of his girl children maybe he would like his son.

When my mother was pregnant, our parents would have intense discussions about my brother's name. My mom didn't want to have a son named "junior." She said that it sounded like the son would always be less than the father. However, my dad's voice would rise when he responded with, *"Having a son with my name is a good family tradition."* They would yell about it for days. Finally, the decision was made. My father's name was William Charles, and my brother's name would be Charles William.

He was such a little cutie with blond hair and pudgy cheeks. I loved him right away. I remember catching tadpoles with him in the cold creek water that flowed through the park located next to our house. He was very adept at catching the tadpoles but was so impatient waiting for them to change into frogs. He would approach the bucket of water containing the creek-caught tadpoles, bend down close, look straight into the bucket and talk to them as only a precocious, young boy can do.

"Hurry up guys. You got to get big so that your legs can help ya' get outs des bucket." For him, time would stand still until he could detect even the slightest change in the tadpoles' appearance. When he did notice the amphibian's change he would jump up and down next to the bucket and wave his arms in the air.

"I see legs, I see legs," he would yell. Their metamorphosis in nature gave my brother pure joy.

****

My brother had another encounter with wildlife that wasn't so positive. My dad's older brother, Otto, had a hunting cabin. It was a rustic retreat that harbored weekend hunters wanting to bag that once-in-a-lifetime trophy and then brag about it for the next five years at every card game that they attend.

One particular weekend our family was invited to just relax at the cabin. My brother, Chuck was about two years old at the time. My uncle reminded us that the cabin had not been used since last year's season and that there may be small creatures running around in the corners.

"Don't crawl on the dirty floors, and don't put anything in your mouth," - my mother's warning was the ruling law. Ignoring the law would definitely carry a consequence.

Of course, this was the signal to explore and investigate every dark nook and cranny of the deserted rooms. Chuck, being a typical two-year old, took total advantage of his few precious moments of freedom. It was much like watching a small wind-up toy with a wound-up spring when he took off. As soon as my mother walked into the cabin and set my brother down on his two small little feet his went into hyper-drive mode and scurried away with split-second timing. When my mom finally caught him, he was covered with fine dust and was chewing on a broken arrow from a homemade bow and arrow set.

Right then and there, my mother decided that we were not spending the night in my uncle's cabin. We drove home and everyone got a super scrub to get rid of all kinds of "who knows what."

The real surprise came the next morning. When I entered the kitchen to eat breakfast, Chuck was sitting in the high chair having his oatmeal. I bent down to kiss him. I touched his soft cheek and ran my hand lightly over his head. I felt a slight rough spot in his hair. I looked at what appeared to be a small, round, brown spot on the top of his head.

"Mom, Chuck has something on his head," I said. She walked over to examine what I found.

"He has a wood tick on his head!" she yelled.

Obviously, this was bad. My mom said that it would suck blood out of my brother's head and that it needed to be taken off immediately. My sweet brother had no idea what all the fuss was over. He was just happy to have someone pay attention to him in a concerned way. My mom proceeded to light up a cigarette. I couldn't imagine why she would be smoking at a time when we needed to get medical attention for my brother.

"If I put heat next to the tick it will release its hold on the skin and back off," she said with authority. My mom puffed and puffed on her cigarette until the tip glowed like an inflamed meteor. She took the cigarette out of her mouth and slowly set the ignited tip ever so close to the imbedded tick.

My brother's attention was promptly focused on the burning fireball etched into his head. His flailing arms grabbed at the stinging, hot poker. My mother immediately restrained him. My brother howled with pain. My mother pressed the glowing end of the cigarette even deeper into the wood tick. It became a revenge battle between my mom and the tick. If you knew my mom, the end was already decided. The tick would surely be defeated. However, my mom seemed to be oblivious to the fact that my little brother was also involved in the encounter. I was sorry that I had even mentioned the presence of the tick. I had to yell at my mom to get her attention and pull at her arm to get her to pull the cigarette away from my brother's head.

"No, mom—hurts! No, mom—hurts! Stop! Stop!" My brother begged as he cried in pain.

Finally, after what seemed to me to be an eternity, my mom reluctantly removed her burning torch. Then, she went to the kitchen cabinet and got a bottle of medicinal alcohol. She trickled it to a cotton ball and applied it to the scorching site atop my brother's head while stating, *"If we starve the oxygen from the tick, he will give up, release his hold, and die."*

All the while, my little brother was again screaming in pain and desperately trying to escape from his high chair. Again, my mom seemed to be oblivious to the pain that was causing my little brother. I was silently praying that the reluctant tick would just give up and die. Possibly my prayers were heard because when my mother attacked the tick's tenuous hold with a pair of tweezers, she was successful in removing it from its embedded entrenchment. She ceremoniously flushed it down the toilet. I never again notified my mother about anything that was out of place in our home or our lives.

****

Other cherished memories revolve around weeding the large garden in our backyard. We all had to participate in garden weeding as a part of our chores. We all despised the chore and would try numerous ways to escape the torture.

One memorable afternoon, when it was particularly hot and muggy, Chuck approached the issue with a very unique solution. All of his previous endeavors to get out of the chore had been futile. Finally, with sweat dripping from his forehead and shoulders, he stood up from his kneeling position, deliberately placed his hands squarely on his hips and announced in a very loud voice in the middle of the pea patch, *"Every part of my body hurts. Even my eye balls hurts."* Well, we all knew this would do no good. True to form - my dad simply told him "get back *to pulling up the weeds and shut up."* I remember thinking it was the most original excuse I had ever heard. I thought that my little brother was a pretty smart little guy.

****

In a Christmas picture of our family taken in 1956, our mother had artificially gathered us around the dining room table. We have smiles on our faces. Our dad is holding a very young Chuck on his lap. This occasion is pretty special because I don't have any other pictures of my dad holding any of us children. It is a rare and cherished picture because as time passed the relationship between our dad and my brother would definitely deteriorate into a mangled kinship. Maybe, at some point my dad actually cared for his son?

I remember another picture taken in August, 1960, during one of our infrequent family trips to Nebraska to visit my mother's family. We are standing outside of my maternal grandparents' house. My dad is actually standing right behind my four-year old brother.

In June, 1963, our parents took us on a rare family trip. My dad bought my brother, Chuck, a hat with the "U.S.S. Admiral" insignia on the front after touring the large boat. The girls in the picture didn't have names on our hats. I have vivid memories of my father when it came to money matters: He never spent a penny that he didn't have to spend. If he spent extra money to purchase a hat with words on it, it was a very big deal. He must have had some special feelings for his son.

In June, 1965, my mother took a picture of our family at dinner in the dining room. We are all seated wearing our dress-up clothes. In the picture, Chuck is setting right next to my dad, in a place of honor. As the years progressed and we became targets of our father's apathy, neglect, and abuse, that position became less desirable. Even though Chuck was sitting in the place of honor at a young age, I never remember my dad giving my brother words of praise or encouragement in school or sporting activities.

I graduated from high school in 1967, attended airline school in 1968, and married in 1969. Therefore, I didn't spend much time at home when Chuck was growing into his teen years. I do remember that he started grade school at Sacred Heart but was transferred to Cathedral School after a few years. I believe that transfer occurred because of a controversy between the nuns at Sacred Heart and my mother. The nuns required that my brother wear a certain type and color of uniform pants to class. Since the issue could not be resolved, my parents transferred Chuck. He attended St. James Trade School for his freshman and sophomore years of high school.

****

Of course, Chuck endured the beatings from our mother as we all had done. The one difference for my brother was that not only was mom beating him but dad as well. I remember talking to my mother later in life about that issue. She was very hesitant to discuss the abuse she had inflicted on us. In fact, she would continually deny that she had ever abused or hit any of her children. I guess that if she pretended that it didn't happen then she felt it didn't happen. However, she did hesitantly share one thing that I will never forget. My mother and I were casually talking about events that occurred when we were growing up. We drifted into discussing Chuck's childhood: How cute he was and how he had a good sense of humor. Inevitably, the discussion turned more serious when I brought up the way dad acted toward Chuck. The tone of her voice changed and her body stiffened.

"One day I realized that we were both beating on the poor little kid," she said. *"It was as if he couldn't do anything right."* She was referring to the fact that both she and dad were beating Chuck for various reasons.

That was a huge and begrudging admission for my mom. Of course, she would not admit to abusing her children without adding the fact that our dad had also taken part in it. It was as if her behavior could be excused her if dad was also beating us.

I know how emotionally devastating the abuse I endured from my mother was. I can only imagine how hurtful, damaging, and painful it must have been for my sweet, little brother to have abuse hurled on him from both parents. I am not talking about a swift little tap on the bottom once in awhile or even on the arm. I am talking about beating with various, available household items and tree branches. I clearly remember these items being used on my siblings and me by my mother. The offenses that invoked this treatment could be as simple as not taking out the household trash at the correct time or failing to put dirty socks in the right basket when they needed to be washed. When I talk with Chuck about his childhood memories, he denies having any memories during that time. I imagine that this is a protective behavior for him since forgetting or denying painful memories is a shield from the abuse.

****

During Chuck's years at St. James Trade School, he took a woodworking class. The project he chose to complete was a wooden jewelry box. By that time, I had married and was living in South Carolina. Still, he sent me the treasured brown wooden box for a birthday gift in 1970. I loved it as soon as I saw it. It had been carefully wrapped, and I knew that Chuck was proud of what he had built just as I was proud to receive it.

Since we were a military family we moved many times in the intervening years. However, with each move, I would gently and carefully pack the brown wooden box to ensure that it would not be damaged. In addition, I always made sure that it was packed with my personal goods and not sent ahead with the household boxes. It was special to me. It came from my brother, who I dearly love.

It is now 2014, 44 years after the precious box was hand crafted and sent to me. It was the first and only time that someone handmade a special gift for me. Even though much care has been taken with the box, the exterior bears a few small nicks and scratches. It stands 7-1/2 inches tall and is 9-3/4 inches wide. The three-drawer cabinet is made of a warm, red-toned wood and topped with an oval mirror. The mirror is encased in the same warm-toned wood. Each of the removable drawers has been lined with a brown-toned, variegated corduroy material. The face of each drawer has a white wooden knob attached in a central location for easy removal. The joints of the drawers and the frame of the box were joined with dovetail construction. It is evident that the box was carefully made with pride. I know that the brown wooden box will last a lifetime.

Over the years, it contained my jewelry and the sacred cows of my life. Every time I look at the box or place a piece of jewelry in the drawer, I am reminded of my precious brother.

****

I believe that one bright path for Chuck was the good education he received at St. James Trade School. However, the administrators of the school closed it after Chuck's sophomore year so he attended Southeast High School for his junior and senior years.

It was during this time that he had one final fight with our dad. I had already left home and was raising a family of my own as a military wife. However, I heard the story of the event from both Chuck and my older sister.

Chuck had a curfew, but on this particular evening, he had come home after the curfew had passed. My dad had intentionally locked all of the doors and windows to prevent him from getting back into the house. However, Chuck was a resourceful teen. He figured out how to get the window in the garage open. He then took off the lock of the door in the garage that opened into the kitchen. When he swung open the kitchen door, he stood face-to-face with dad, who was dressed in his robe and flustered with fury. Dad was ready to challenge Chuck and punish him yet again. I am sure that my dad saw this as a major challenge to his authority.

The two of them faced each other for a murderous moment in the dark kitchen. Then dad shoved Chuck on the shoulders and began yelling at him. Chuck shoved him right back, just as hard. Dad shoved again, this time harder. Chuck returned the action. The shoving and pushing escalated from both directions with each man bearing his fists and posturing. Their eyes locked in hatred, stabbing gazes, their actions were finally solidified.

Resolve congealed into action. Again dad pushed hard on Chuck's chest, but when my brother returned the deed, my dad went flying across the kitchen and landed on top of the kitchen table, sliding into a chair. Table and chair both sustained damage. As my dad lay crumpled on the broken chair, he sat stunned for a moment. Then he began yelling for my enraged brother to leave the house and never return. Needless to say, my brother left home that night, forever!

For the next couple of weeks, Chuck slept in his car in the parking lot of Southeast High School. It was winter time and, surely, bitterly cold outside. He was eventually able to arrange for sleeping quarters in a friend's spare bedroom. I am certain that the survival skills that my brother unfortunately had to develop during this intense and lonely time served him well later in life when he faced difficult situations. I am also certain that he felt betrayed, scared, hurt, and confused.

My mom stood by and watched this bitter family fight, making no attempt to protect her son or persuade my dad to soften his approach. I believe that my sweet brother became a man that evening—much too soon. I truly regret that I was not in the house that evening. Had I been present, I would have stood by Chuck and helped him ward off the attack. My dad was a mean, hateful, and vengeful man. I can only imagine the bravery it took for my brother to stand up to him.

The reason I recount these few youthful interactions of my brother is to explain his enduring personality and the intense and intimidating surroundings in which he spent his formative years. He is a son, he is the brother of many sisters, but most importantly he is my little, loving brother.

When I have finished reminiscing about the past, I carefully lift the brown wooden box from the shelf and remove the protective wrap. I had covered it to keep it safe. Opening the drawers, I find a collection of items that represent different aspects of my life.

I focus on a small black and white china dog that is posed in a playful position. Its white body is capped with black ears, paws, and tail. The minute figurine was once in a china cabinet in my Aunt Annie's house. She was one of my dad's younger sisters. She was a poorly educated "spinster" who worked as a cleaning woman for F. L. Insurance Company.

She told me that the front room of a house was special because it is where a person receives and entertains guests. She always placed her most valued possessions in the china cabinet in the front room. When we would visit my aunt, I would always hurry to view the cherished articles within the case. The little china dog always sat in the front in a place of honor. Receiving the small china dog during an overnight stay with my aunt was a memorable moment. I'm not sure why I got to stay with my aunt on that particular night, but I don't believe that any of my sisters got the same privilege.

My Aunt Annie shared a home with her brother, Benjamin or Uncle Benny as I called him. He was my father's older brother and also unmarried. Uncle Benny was an alcoholic and a womanizer in his younger years. Aunt Annie told me a story about Uncle Benny's childhood that explained his poor behavior.

My dad and his twelve siblings grew up next P. Brick Company. It was a large building that used quantities of wet, muddy shale and sand to produce bricks. These products were used in erecting Springfield's fire stations, churches and state buildings. Often, when the factory was closed for the evening, my dad and uncles would sneak in a back window to look for the left over wet brick clay. They could shape the moist material into small, round marbles that provided them with hours of enjoyment.

During one of these forbidden adventures, Uncle Benny climbed on one of the big machines to get the sticky stuff instead of picking it off of the factory floor. He slipped into the machine, head first. He hit his head and was knocked unconscious for a long time. My dad and his brothers had to pull him out of the machine. They struggled to pass him back through the window and smuggled him home before their parents discovered the dastardly deed.

Uncle Benny recovered very slowly and was different after the fall. My aunt said that when he regained consciousness, he couldn't remember things or add up numbers like he had been able to do before he had hit his head. Also, he didn't feel comfortable in social settings and wasn't able to interact with people whereas before the accident he had been a very likable and social child.

By the time he reached adulthood, unsavory adults were able to take advantage of him. Often, they convinced him to spend his entire paycheck at the local bar and stay out for days at a time without notifying any family members. His sisters and brothers decided that it would be best for him to live with Aunt Annie. She volunteered to keep his out of trouble. That is how Aunt Annie and Uncle Benny came to live together for the rest of their lives. They didn't have any problems that I could detect. Both were secured menial employment and supported themselves until their death. They helped each other to balance out the others' world.

Remembering the societal attitudes toward single adults helped to shape my perspective about my aunt and uncle. Generally, it was acceptable for a man to be a bachelor for life and earn a living. However, there seemed to be an unwritten law against older women being unmarried and earning a living on her own. Even the term given her, old maid, attributed a sense of degradation to her status.

During that stay with Aunt Annie and Uncle Benny, I also received my paternal great-grandfathers' passport from my aunt. My great-grandfather acquired this document in 1890 when he secured passage from Germany on a ship named Ems (Lake Simcoe Ship). It was then that he entered the United States of America with his wife, daughter, and seventeen year old son, Otto, who would become my grandfather. The green, paper document was inscribed with official words written in the German language. It indicated that his name was Ludwig Götschenberger, and he had come from Katchenthal, Germany. The third page contained entries for his wife and children: Maria (Lell) born May 17, 1847, their daughter, Anna, born November 1, 1867, and my grandfather, Otto, born April 3, 1873.

Once I discovered it existed, I knew that I would bargain almost anything to obtain the booklet. I still can't explain the feeling, but I knew, even then, that I would use the treasured family heirloom later in life to attach my family past with present day events of my life. My aunt and I had a discussion about it, but finally, she gave in to my pleading. I received the passport! In exchange for the special gift, she elicited a promise from me not to tell my siblings that she had given me the prized book–it was our special secret.

Having a special secret with someone bonds you to that person. Everyone who keeps a secret automatically attains a heightened status in society. At least, that is how it seems to me. I never divulged the covert information I shared with my aunt until I was an adult. By then, after her death, the telling of the secret was anticlimactic. However, during the bartering session to obtain my great- grandfather's passport, it seemed as if it were the most important secret I had ever had to keep.

It made me feel special that an adult would trust me enough with it and with some of our cherished family history. I am still surprised that she said yes. I have shared the passport with my granddaughter. Someday, if she is able to keep a secret really well, I may give it to her.

Next to these items in the wooden box is a 1-inch square brass, hinged box with the initials "F.R." inscribed on the top of the lid. On the inside, it is divided into multiple sections. The box is about 80 years old. Seeing it reminds me of a conversation I had with my mother a few years before her death. She told me that this small, brass inscribed case was a pillbox belonging to her father, Fred Ruser. He was from Wakefield, Nebraska. He would use the container to carry his medication when he was attending a formal or special public occasion or when he went on a business trip. I remember my grandfather was short in stature with a barrel shaped chest. He always smelled like cigars. His salt and pepper hair was perpetually greased with a hair tonic that smelled like Aqua Velva. My maternal grandfather, Fred Ruser, died in 1967 following a car accident from a blood clot in his brain. I wonder if he had the pillbox in his pocket and if he were traveling to a business meeting.

Beside the brass box is a tarnished, silver thimble that belonged to my maternal grandmother, Meta (Lilje) Ruser. It is perforated with multiple indentations on the top that represent the thousands of needle impressions from my grandmother's hand sewing sessions. I'm sure that she spent many an evening after the harvest was complete and the canning done, sitting in a chair in the front room repairing her husband's and children's clothing. She was a farm wife who assisted her husband with all the farm chores and also tended to the household duties. I remember her referring to her sewing, knitting, and crocheting as doing her "fancy work." As I hold the tarnished thimble in my hands, her essence fills the room. My grandmother may have used the thimble to make some of the fine lace doilies that grace my living room. She died in 1989. She was a kind, gentle, loving lady who didn't speak often but when she did her words were thoughtful pearls of wisdom. I miss her!

****

In the middle drawer are three tarnished silver necklaces of differing sizes. These were purchased with funds from my first paycheck after receiving my associate degree in nursing from the University of Hawaii. It was the first time I had bought something special just for me. I rewarded myself by buying additional silver chains when I graduated with my Bachelor's degree in Nursing. It was an extravagant expense since I had bills to pay and groceries to buy for my three little children. Feeling a little selfish, I secretly splurged on myself. I still reminisce about how nice it would have been if my husband had given me some small trinket of acknowledgement. He was irritated on the day of my graduation because he had to take care of our children during the commencement ceremony. It was warm in Hawaii that day, and the campus seemed to be filled with graduation activity. He didn't want to bother with his family.

As I quickly clean away the tarnish, the necklaces are restored to their former luster. Looking at them in their restored, shiny state stirs the wonderful memories of my life in Hawaii. I can't resist placing them around my neck and looking at them in the mirror. They are comforting and fill me with a cozy, warm reminder of my accomplishments.

In with the silver chains is a collection of sand dollars that I collected when we lived in Charleston, South Carolina. One is decorated and dated. It has a small picture of a dog on the front and the back reads: "B. Z. 1979." This memento is from my son, Brian. He made it when he was nine years old. It also has a bit of red and green felt attached to the back. I think it may originally have been on a Christmas card. Brian is now forth-three years old.

****

Another drawer contains a glass container, two inches square, that was given to me by the W. Hospital management staff. It was a token gift for Nurses' Appreciation Day in Sacramento, California in the 1980's. Looking over all the physical reminders of my years of healthcare dedication are, a glass container, a worn out stethoscope, a penlight that never worked when I really needed it, and multiple pairs of worn-out nursing shoes. I realize that the outward rewards of the profession are skeletal although my memories are rich and varied. Sadly, whenever I try to share the rich experiences or to relate the lessons I have learned, no one is interested. I experience a moment of sadness and melancholy at this thought.

The drawers continue to reveal family memories. Inside the glass container is a collection of small, round, embossed pictures of my three children. They show Erica as a baby, Tarena as a toddler, and Brian as a boy in elementary school in Hawaii. Each series of pictures is encased in a charm that was made to attach to a bracelet. These were promotional items from the companies employed to take school pictures. Smiling, I remember watching my children grow and mature while we relocated to different military bases across the United States. My husband's multiple transfers exposed my children to many different cultures and experiences. It gave them a social, interactive education that was more valuable than any they could have received from simply reading a book.

The bottom drawer contains a few American silver dollars dating from 1969 thru 2000. As I examine the coins, I realize they are really a sandwich of alloy metals. As the dates progress forward there is less and less pure material in each coin. The coin, dated 2000, shows a replica of Sacajawea carrying a small baby. This coin is the most discolored with a patina of copper, blue, and silver, which I wipe away. Like my necklace, these coins remind me that although I collect the tarnish of life's experiences, I can go forward to better days with a little polish just like Sacajawea did when she lead Lewis and Clark across the entangled, uncharted wilderness.

The last item in the drawer is a wristwatch. The illuminated background outlines the numbered dial with an hour, minute, and second hand. It's the last wristwatch I ever wore. I removed from my right wrist when I completed my last day of hospital nursing. The hands no longer rotate since the battery needs to be replaced. The hands stopped moving at two minutes after 5 O'clock. I took it off of my wrist because I finally was in control of my time and my nursing career. I have not used a wristwatch since that day. I may put a new battery in it someday, but not today.

As I look over all of the heirlooms I keep inside my brown wooden box, I am pleased. The box, crafted by my brother, has faithfully held my sacred cows and precious jewelry for many years. It certainly stood the test of time—just like my relationship with my beloved brother. The brown wooden box is just one of the many precious treasures that he has given to me.

Chuck has dedicated his life to serving in the government. He has given many others a lifelong gift: friendship and leadership from a reputable government. He currently holds the position of State Representative for the State of Missouri. He has been in this position for the past six years. He demonstrates that same pure joy that I witnessed when he observed the change in the tadpoles waiting for transformation in the bucket. Finally, through a hard-won struggle, they received their legs and could hop out of the confines of the bucket. The value of change for the better is ingrained in Chuck. He has demonstrated that aspect of happiness when he ushers a bill through the political process and it changes into law. Chuck knows that a good law is good for the people. He helps them to stands on the firm ground of good government.

The same perseverance that he used for survival when he was thrown out of our dad's house has helped Chuck develop a successful life and climb the political ladder. He has realized that he has inner abilities that can be used to secure resources to make positive change occur. Examples such as: truly extending his hand in friendship, being alert to the dangers of public corruption and having the courage to fight against it, and working together with others when it is obvious that things are easier to complete when the job is approached from a group perspective. These talents occur within Chuck naturally. He was born with them. He was given the skills and Chuck has the intelligence and the personal courage to develop that flair. He understands that truly "one person does make a difference." It's obvious that Chuck has made that difference both in his life and the life of his community. The people of Missouri are thankful for good, honest leadership.

My thankfulness comes from owning the treasured brown wooden box. Periodically removing it from the shelf and touching its treasures always provides a mental base for me. Having such a well-crafted memory holder would be a valuable prize for anyone. However, having a brother like Chuck is far superior.

Chapter 8

The In-Laws

My mother-in-law had decided that no girl would ever be good enough to marry her son long before I came into the picture. She often referred to her youngest child as her "little Billy Boy."

She had planned out the lives of all her children. They would only marry approved spouses and then have children after settling in a wood-framed home next to mom and dad in their quiet bucolic setting. Three generations of my husband's family lived within five miles of his house, and his mother had determined that the trend should continue. He was the baby in his family and had been loved, cherished, coddled, and excused all of his life until I entered the picture. My challenge was that I didn't understand this when I fell in love with Bill.

In the late '60's, Bill had completed his first year of junior college and was deciding between the Air Force and the Army for military duty. "Uncle Sam was hot on his trail." We met on a Saturday at the local drive-in movie theatre under unusual circumstances. It was a girl's –night out for me and a couple of friends from my all-girls private high school. I'm sure that driving my dad's green station wagon didn't set us apart for any entertaining excitement the night. Bill's car, full of guys, parked next to ours. It was packed with his rowdy male relations who started talking and yelling.

"*This movie is awful,*" they shouted out their car window. "*Come on let's get out of here!*"

"*We're bored, let's get some chow up at the shack, and then we'll leave.*"

The girls and I decided that we also needed to leave. We couldn't enjoy the movie with all that shouting anyway. We wanted to stay, though, until the guys left their car to go to the concession stand so they wouldn't follow us. While we waited, we joked that the guys were just a bunch of rude hillbillies that probably didn't even know how to read.

Finally, they opened their car doors, got out and headed for the concession stand. Unfortunately, as soon as I started the engine of the car and put it into gear, we were startled by the sound of our own car doors opening. Instead of going to the concession stand, as they had stated, the boys scurried around the back of their car, opened the back doors of our car and jumped inside. They started yelling and screaming about how terrible themovie was while they piled into our vehicle. In the midst of the chaos, they said that they thought that they had met us somewhere before... *Ha! Ha!*

They introduced themselves by first names only and said that they were all related.

"Get out of the car!" we all yelled in unison.

"Not until you drive us to Small Town," they answered in unison.

Not only did I not want to meet their silly request, I had no idea where this "Small Town" place was. *"Get out of the car!"* I commanded, raising the tone of my voice and pointing my finger into the air. I just wanted to get the hell out of there and never see these spooky guys again. They just looked at each other and laughed. A sick feeling occupied my stomach: maybe we were all in real trouble. For a moment I imagined in my minds' eye all three of us girls lying dead on a deserted road.

"I don't have enough gas to drive to Small Town. Besides, this is my dad's car and he expects it back in the drive within a half hour of the movie ending." I said with as firm a tone as I could muster.

"We'll buy all the gas, baby," they said cheerfully.

Somehow, I sensed that this dialogue could and would go on for hours. I felt that these boys were accustomed to getting their way. We girls, who were all sitting in the front seat, huddled and quietly discussed our options. We finally decided to drive these goofy guys to Small Town. There, we would throw them out of the car onto the road and drive away.

Of course, we knew that we were putting ourselves into danger. It could be the night that we were killed and never seen again. If our lifeless bodies ended up in a concealed area, our parents and friends would never know what happened to us. We would be found dead on a dark, deserted road.

Begrudgingly, we drove this group of guys to Small Town. They talked and joked during the entire trip – which took about thirty minutes. During the drive they asked for our names. I foolishly repeated my real name. I did it quickly, thinking they would never remember it because it was so long and difficult to pronounce.

Surprisingly, Bill called me two weeks later. He introduced himself as the *"guy who lives in Small Town and was with his relatives at the drive-in."* He said that he forgot my last name and it took him two weeks to find it in the telephone book. Eventually, he just looked for the longest last name in the directory and called it – I just happened to answer the call.

I decided this guy was fairly resourceful, and so we met again and started dating on a regular basis. I eventually learned that not only Bill but also all of the guys in the car that evening at the drive-in were normal young men and indeed related. Bill enlisted in the Air Force a few months later. I graduated from high school and went to airline school. We decided to invest time and telephone lines in a long distance relationship.

True love and marriage at that time was uncertain. It was a strange way to start a romantic relationship. Our drive-in incident marked the beginning of the pathway of my in-law interactions.

The first time that I met my sister-in-laws was memorable- they had green hair. Bill and I were going to a party, and he suggested that we stop by his house to meet them on the way. When we walked into the kitchen, his older twin sisters were in the process of changing their hair color. They were sitting on chairs and had their heads wrapped in towels. Approaching them to say "hello" caused them to stand up which is when the towels fell from their heads, revealing their green-colored hair. They explained that they had not read the directions on the box and, as a result hadn't followed all the steps in the dying process. They were trying to change their hair color from brown to blond–they got green.

Outside the house, Bill apologized for taking me to meet his family without letting everyone know that I was coming. Something told me that he was going to have to answer to two angry sisters when he got back home.

His sisters soon revealed their true feelings toward me as I spent more time at their family home and as it became apparent that I would marry their baby brother. They shared their mother's attitude that no woman was good enough for their little brother. Even if Princess Diana had been their brother's choice, they would have found fault.

As my relationship with my soon to-be-husband progressed, he proposed and we set the marriage date. However, the military also set the date for his transfer to another air force base in Texas. We continued our long-distance engagement. If we had been smart, we would have invested in the Bell telephone system at that point. Our long distance daily phone calls would have provided enough financial proceeds for us to build a large bank account with which to start our wedded bliss.

Since I was in Kansas attending airline school and Bill was in basic training in Texas, we quickly developed a routine. Nightly phone calls contained a review of the days' activities, future plans, and expressions of affection. After being engaged for two years, we set a wedding date. However, since I was Catholic and wanted to be married in the church and Bill attended a Protestant Church, my church required that he complete a pre-nuptial marriage class at the Catholic Church where he was stationed. He agreed to this without too much concern.

Unfortunately, his mother was furious and vocal with the situation. She was strictly against her son changing his religion or being exposed to any religion of which she did not approve: she definitely didn't approve and this situation was unacceptable.

Her reaction and her influence over her son threatened to ruin our wedding plans and certainly influenced our marriage. Despite the intense opposition, Bill completed the pre-nuptial class and we were married in the Catholic faith amidst continued protests. This gave me hope that he may be able to stand on his own two feet as an adult and decide his future even if it were in opposition to his mother's wishes.

His mother's intense opinion and philosophy were jointly shared by his older sisters in all things. Sundays were for family dinners around the dining room table, and weekends were spent doing household chores: Tuesdays were laundry days; Mondays were house cleaning days; Thursdays were for paying the bills. There would be no exceptions.

Bill and I often discussed this rigid regime from his childhood. We needed to establish our own family traditions. Afraid that he wasn't truly bonding with me and involved in our family commitments, I reserved my strong opinions on this subject until we had a chance to build our relationship on firm ground. Regrets followed me concerning this decision for all of my married life because bonding and firm ground seemed to be illusive throughout our relationship. This lack of commitment from my husband was a central issue in our problems. It wove through the tapestry of our marriage. Bill consistently seemed to be unable to psychologically separate from his mother in a healthy manner. I didn't realize it at the beginning of our marriage but the presence of, and the interference into, our lives by the in-laws would ultimately be at the heart of the destruction of our lives together.

Naïvely, we did marry and became a military family. We formed a preliminary relationship based on trying to please the other partner and not on true and abiding love for each other. This triad of husband, wife, and in-laws was built on shaky ground.

My husband's true allegiance was always to his mother and family of birth. The initial four years of our marriage were spent on a military duty assignment in South Carolina. This offered us an opportunity to develop an initial relationship away from his family. However, Bill was never able to make a complete commitment to the family that we created. The years passed and, every time we had a chance for a vacation, it always involved a trip to his parent's home. Whenever we had a wonderful event occur in our family (i.e. birthday, christening, birth or educational achievement), Bill would quickly run to the telephone to inform his parents first before he would attend or enjoy the event with our family.

Bill's mother reveled in the role of matriarch. She would yield it as a dagger, sword, hatchet, or shovel – whatever the occasion required. She was the will of the family and all yielded to her opinion or their life was extremely difficult. Bill's mom did not like me as a daughter-in-law, and she made no bones about showing me or anyone else her opinion. The sole role I played, in her family view, was to give her grandchildren. In that capacity, I was tolerated. She would become very irritated when I influenced her son in making decisions of which she did not approve. Along came Joyce and threw a monkey wrench into her domineering attitude. My mother-in-law was angry!

She easily enlisted the extended family into her plan to win her son's total obedience. She systemically invited some family members to pass around nasty information concerning my family and me. It made our daily life stressful and difficult. I quickly learned that if our marriage was to survive, we needed to physically live far away from Bill's mom.

I was extremely eager to encourage Bill to extend his initial time in the U.S. Air Force. This would require that Bill and I would have to rely on each other to care for our family, and would not be able to physically interact with Bill's mother on a daily basis. This helped Bill slowly to separate physically and I hoped psychologically from his mother's domination in a healthy manner. I thought that it would also help him to make a total commitment to our family and our marriage. It took me thirty-five years to realize that ultimately that was not to be.

Bill spent twenty-two years in the Air Force, and we traveled around the United States from Hawaii to South Carolina. Still, there was always an undercurrent hovering silently around us. The unspoken understanding emitting from Bill was: *"We will go back home to live with mom when I retire."* He just wouldn't cut the strings. He couldn't stand alone as an independent adult male at the head of his own family.

However, Bill's own father was a partial role model for his son. My father-in-law was an understanding, caring, helpful, quiet, good human being. He just wanted people to be happy and to live a simple life. He didn't take risks or rock the boat. Unfortunately, he paid dearly for his philosophy. Living with a hard-crusted, self-indulgent woman meant that this man had to sacrifice much of life's pleasures.

I liked and loved Bill's dad as soon as I met him. He was unassuming and welcoming. He made eye contact while shaking my hand. I felt as if he understood that I could help his son face life with direction and intention. I almost wished that he were a much younger man, a man who could understand me. However, he had already spent many years under the yoke of a hard, willful, domineering woman when we first met, and his potential for greatness had faded. He was not the decision maker in his family.

He had been a man of strong character and obvious integrity. He was a gifted teacher. I observed his interactions and could learn each aspect of any new task under his loving watchfulness. However, he was now simply my father-in-law.

Bill's dad died of lung cancer when Bill was on military station with the Air Force in Hawaii. It was a very sad day for our family. I knew that we had lost the only soft hearted, loving person in our linage. Bill's mom was also diagnosed with lung cancer a few years after Bill had retired from active duty. After a lengthy discussion, Bill and I decided to take an extended leave from our jobs and travel to Illinois and care for her. I hoped that this would give family members a chance to smooth over the tense and rough edges that had been so obvious in all of our interactions. While we were caring for his mother, we volunteered to work on the needed repairs to her home.

This commitment involved extensive physical labor and attention to the detailed around-the-clock monitoring of Bill's mother's hospice needs. Once the house was in order, following the death of Bill's mother, Bill and I had time to reflect on our lives together. I hoped for a time of marital closeness and mutual support. However, that was not to be.

I overheard a conversation involving one of Bill's sisters in which she said Bill and I were considered free loaders since we didn't pay rent while we were living in the family home. I guess that caring for Bill's mother and physically upgrading their home did not excuse us from paying for the privilege of living there.

Bill also made several verbal remarks to his sisters that he didn't think that I was fully invested in working on house repairs. In other words, he hinted to his family that I wanted to get paid for helping his dying mother and refurbishing her house. I was mortified, embarrassed, and insulted. This was totally false. Bill always knew how to hurt me in the worst, most stinging ways – to me, this verbal falsehood obviously reinforced where his allegiance remained. I wonder why I was reluctant to approach Bill and discuss our degrading relationship. Maybe, I thought that he was grieving for the loss of his mother. Possibly, I was scared that our union would not hold up under the examination. Could it be that I was afraid of the approaching dissolution of our marriage?

****

My final release from the marital baggage that I accepted from my husband came during his own funeral process. Even though I had endured the pain of my life partner's marital humiliation, I was honor bound to fulfill his last wish – burial in a veteran's cemetery near his home town.

I arranged for the internment at Camp Butler after we had an intimate memorial ceremony at our family church in Pahrump, Nevada. The church community in this small, desert town embraced us and offered solace and support during this very devastating period. The service fortified my children and me for our final meeting with the people who had ruled our lives even at a distance – and when that wasn't enough had shown up on our door step, uninvited, to intervene.

My sisters and brother opened their homes and hearts to our family's arrival in Illinois. We stayed with "Ant Lan's," but all my siblings accompanied us to the burial site. Emotions were intense – palpating like microwaves cooking a raw slab of beef. I was satisfied and comforted with the burial arrangements completed through the Veteran's Administration. My children and I intentionally arrived at the cemetery just a few minutes prior to the ceremony - under a cloudy sky. Somehow the weather seemed to match our mood. We didn't relish the idea of a face-to-face contact with any of the in-laws under these circumstances.

My husband, their father, was being laid to rest with so many unanswered questions. Bill seemed so reluctant to talk with me about intimate issues as he was dying even though I encouraged him to do so. Something had been bothering him before his death but yet he fought to keep it a secret. We could only wonder. My mind was focused and pre-occupied on these secrets as I approached the front row of the funeral seating in the cemetery site.

Stunningly, but perhaps not surprisingly, I noticed Bill's sister and cousin's from the corner of my eye. They had strategically positioned themselves directly behind my appointed chair which was positioned next to my children. The thought flashed through my brain that my in-laws was here to drive me away to a small, deserted hideaway, again. I frantically searched the crowd for the protective faces of my siblings. Thankfully, finding my brothers' gaze, he acknowledged my desire and physically occupied a protective stance. It had not been the first time my brother had helped and protected me and my family.

I was numb to the surroundings or other attendees at the burial ceremony. The seat could have been cold I wouldn't have shivered. The rain could have been heavy I wouldn't have been aware of the moisture on my shoulders. The birds could have been singing clearly I wouldn't have recognized the song. The traffic may have been whizzing by I wouldn't have noticed. Nothing could break through the numbing cocoon which enveloped me.

My eyes scrutinized the black urn containing the ashes of my dead husband setting on the table in front of me until it slowly melted into the red curtain behind it. The curtain moved slightly forward, toward me. My body couldn't feel and my ears couldn't hear but my eyes were experiencing the intense illusion that immovable objects were indeed moving toward me with an unexplainable, unrestrained, paralyzing power. My voice refused to alert others that they needed to stop the forward movement of the red curtain. Every fiber of my being silently screamed that the curtain was going to crush me.

The curtain totally encapsulated the urn and had moved inches from my face. It would not be denied its' pray. There was no explaining the situation. I was going to be consumed by the red curtain that had already devoured my dead husband – I sat resolved to the inevitable. The deed was nearly complete when a nagging voice whispered in my ear – *"Couldn't others at the internment ceremony see the curtain?" Why wasn't someone stopping the curtain?* I turned my head and noticed that my children sat solemnly without care or concern for the devouring red curtain. I didn't understand. I panicked that they were unaware. We were all going to die at my husband's funeral.

Instantly, my ears flooded with waves of noise intermixed with words and music. The red curtain disappeared just at the very instant that it was touching my left cheek. I was jolted back to reality and realized in an instant that the ceremony was complete and the military representative was walking toward me to present the American flag. I was stunned with numbness but automatically extended my arms to receive the honored symbol.

The minister approached me, touched my shoulder and extended terms of sympathy. The mourners began leaving the site. I stood up and numbly walked to my brother's waiting car. It was the only source of solitude that my brain recognized. It wasn't until we later arrived at my sister's house that my thoughts focused on my children and granddaughter. Thankfully, my protective siblings had tended to their safety.

It's obvious that the red curtain at the cemetery site could not physically move or overcome and consume my husband's urn positioned on the ceremony table. If the curtain had been moving, the other attendees would surely have noticed it and would have reacted with fight and amazement as I had done. My frightening experience with the curtain was obviously a reaction to intense and overwhelming stress that I was experiencing from the presence of my in-laws. I believe that my psyche was trying to protect me from an imminent danger – one that I didn't overtly realize. I had rationalized that I would be physically safe in an open area, surrounded by a multitude of people in a socially recognized sacred area. I guess that my psyche didn't perceive the situation in the same manner. I am glad that there is a section of my psychological being that functions to protect me from danger when I'm not consciously aware of the need.

I fulfilled any obligations owed to my husband. I could now thankfully be released from the connection to his family, forever.

Returning home - a burden lifted from my soul - I was reviewing my late husband's paperwork and discovered his marital betrayal. It may have been this morale deceit that he struggled to conceal on his death bed – a secret that the in-laws may have known.

wedding picture of Otto Joseph (seated) and
Magdalena (Stiern) (standing) Gatschenberger

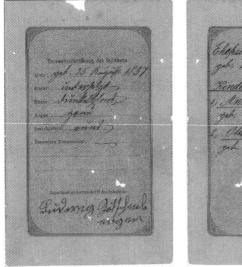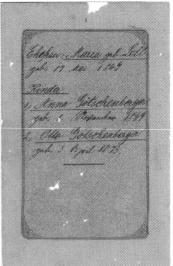

It is a copy of my great-grandfather's passport which he used
when he came into the United States from Germany

Lake Simcoe Ship

ship that brought Ludwig and Mary (Lell) Gatschenberger
along with son Otto Joseph and Anna to America

We five siblings as youngsters - I am standing at far right.

trip on U.S.S. Admiral - Chuck wearing his
monogram hat - I am standing at far left.

Our parents 25th wedding anniversary - I am standing back row, middle

young B and I

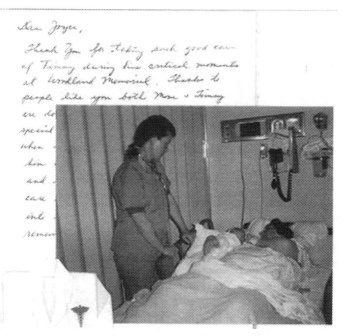

Me and my nursing career

We siblings as adults - I am second from the left.

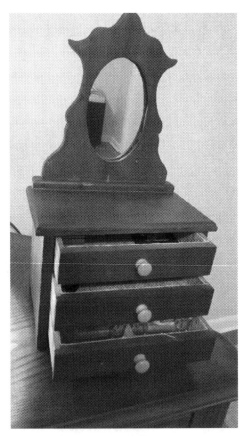

Brown Wooden Box

Tarena and Kiyah

Children and grandchild when Van and I wed

Van and I

Chapter 9

Bri-Bri

He was such a little cutie – blond hair, bright blue eyes, pudgy cheeks and a beaming smile packaged into a bundle of energy. Our first-born child was a joy and ready to make his mark on the world from the moment of his birth. It was the 70's. Brian was born with curiosity, intelligence, and stubbornness. Life would challenge him in many ways, and he would psychologically butt heads when he couldn't control or figure out an issue on his first attempt. Even though he pretended not to love the smothering hugs and kisses from me, I knew that he secretly treasured them. He would curl up his lip and say, *"yuck"* every time came toward him with an affectionate bear hug and a smoochy embrace. I gave him a nickname that seemed to fit him and his personality, Bri-Bri. He would try so hard to pretend that he was a little man.

He wanted the whole world to bend to his will. This was very evident on a family trip to the beach in South Carolina. We had spent a lovely afternoon building sandcastles on the shore. The time was coming in and getting closer and closer to the edge of our valued structures. Brian started building a wall to prevent the sea from destroying his masterpieces. Well, this was a predetermined outcome. The waves soon overcame the first lovingly built castle.

Brian believed that he could deliver a unique solution so that future destruction could be avoided. He abandoned his recovery efforts and stood up with his staunch posture facing the destructive water. He placed his hands on his hips, set a determined stare on his young face and uttered only one forceful word, *"move."* He had total faith that his verbal order would change the tides of the ocean and thereby save his hard-built sandcastles.

I stood and marveled at his determination and stubbornness, knowing that if he could learn to channel those attributes in the right endeavor, he could accomplish almost any endeavor he attempted. He certainly had a tremendous amount of potential. As a mother, I hoped that I could guide him in the right direction. I knew that I had to mix just the right amount of physical love and tenderness with equal amounts of stern discipline.

"You are my one and only little love," I would remind him. He yearned to hear that. In fact, he took it to heart. When his little sisters were added to our family, he was very upset and asked why they had come to live with us.

He approached me when I brought each of them home. Looking me square in the eye, he said, *"You said that I was the one. Now there are more. I don't like it. Take her back."* Each time, he was not easily soothed when he learned that his little sisters were going to stay.

Brian's quick wit and inquisitive mind was no match for his school teachers. He usually grasped his work quickly and moved on to more exciting adventures. The computer age was upon us, and Brian took to it like a fish to water. He would take a computer apart just to see how it worked. He instinctively understood the inner workings of machinery and went to work on a project to modify any program that he could find.

A particular incident concerning his first car is memorable. Instead of taking it to a repair shop, he decided that he would complete the repairs himself. So, on a weekend he pushed the car into our family garage and set up a portable movie camera next to it. He filmed himself taking apart the section of the engine that needed repair. He then replayed the film and fixed the car just like it was new. Monday morning he was able to drive the repaired car out of the garage and down the road.

Brian's inquisitive nature also led him into dangerous territory. He became interested in explosives and gunpowder but was much too fascinated with the dangerous side of these incendiary devices. In his teen years, he began fabricating guns parts from various pieces of metal. He also experimented with mixing and matching various forms of powder in metal projectiles. He seemed to garner satisfaction from developing more combustible mixtures and increasingly intense explosive eruptions.

I began to sense that Brian was acting out some internal unresolved anger or frustration. As he devoted more time toward working with explosives, he became more reclusive, secluding himself from family members and the general public. He became less interactive in everyday activities and less talkative with his former childhood friends. His senior year in high school was the pinnacle of this disparaging activity.

When we received the telephone call from a school counselor one day, it was expected. Brian had been in science class and was completing an assignment using potentially dangerous substances. Of course, with Brian if a little bang was good then a big bang was even better. The counselor reported that Brian had significantly increased the amount of ingredients and the resulting reaction had blown a window out in the science room at the high school. Unfortunately, Brian was quite proud of his accomplishment and saw little need for concern. I remember his response, *"Ah, mom, it sure was fun. I didn't think that it was going to really blow out all of the glass."*

Things were obviously getting out of hand. Following a discussion between the principal, school counselor, Brian, my husband, and me, it was decided that Brian would pay to replace the window and be under close supervision while in the school lab. He would be required to sign out his ingredients from the science teacher for each and every lab period until the end of the school year. Brian hated being under the watchful eye of adults, but he soon learned to buckle under and decrease his interest in explosions, at least while he was at school.

Over the next few months, Brian decided to take his pent up energy out physically by riding his bicycle around the neighborhood. People would observe him riding so fast down the sidewalk or side street they would swear that he was moving like greased lightin'. Brian would ride everywhere for long periods at a time. There was some strong energy within him that was driving him to exert large amounts of energy. If he couldn't expend it by exploding objects, then he would exhaust himself by riding his bicycle to physical exhaustion.

I often imagined that Brian had some inner conflict perhaps relating to some unresolved grief or an issue that kept haunting him. I would ask him why he was so full of rage or intensity, but he would just shake his head and refuse to talk to me. I guess that it is not comfortable for a teenage boy to discuss private things with his mother.

Brian and his father were actively involved in the Boy Scout program. He had many meetings and projects that kept him active and integrated with the community. We thought that this activity would offer him the outlet that he needed to disperse some of his intensity. He seemed to enjoy scouting activities and achieved the rank of Eagle Scout. However, even this didn't seem to quell his intense ardor.

Brian was equally adept at competing in fencing competitions. He participated in statewide programs and placed very high in the rankings. This required that he maintain his concentration and diligence. He also needed to follow the set of rules and regulations governing this centuries-old sporting competition. Fencing was physically demanding and offered an outlet for his energy. During this time he was involved in the sport, he appeared more focused in his daily life.

Brian's adult years saw him retreat more and more from involvement with his community. He also interacted less at our family activities. He was reluctant to attend holiday gatherings or celebrations. Gun smithing and the cloistered professionals involved in the trade became his life.

Because it's a closed community with a dubious reputation, he quickly came under the scrutiny of multiple law enforcement agencies. He and his gun smithing colleagues would often skirt the law by maintaining a watchfulness that bordered on paranoia toward all law enforcement officials. Each new incident would usher in a new wave of paranoia throughout the group.

Unfortunately, as time passed Brian grew into manhood and carried an aura of mistrust toward most law officers. He slowly receded from our close family unit. Fatefully, his dad was diagnosed with terminal cancer. His sisters and I called Brian to inform him of his father's medical condition. We let him know that his father's status was terminal, and we advised him to come for a visit and talk with his dad. Surprisingly, he didn't believe our information and didn't respond to our pleas or requests. It took multiple requests and constant reassurance that his fathers' condition was terminal before he came to visit.

When he entered our house, he was surprised to see a hospice-centered home. His father's bed had been moved into the living room so that he could be an integral part of family activities. The bed was surrounded by medical equipment that supported his father's failing body. I am confident that this unexpected scene was overwhelming to Brian. He may have expected to see his dad sitting up in a chair watching his favorite TV program or talking on the telephone to a friend. Seeing his fragile father languishing in a semi-comatose state was shocking to him. At the time, the hospice nurse was adding a medically ordered morphine to the I.V. line. This medication is often used for comfort and pain management with hospice patients. It often signals a downward direction toward sustaining life functions. Brian entered our home when it was obvious that his father was dying.

Additionally, Brian's aunt had positioned herself at her brother's bedside, and she had no intention of leaving. Even if Brian had wanted to sit quietly to talk with his father about personal issues, he wouldn't have been able to since she was an ever-present, rapacious figure.

This profound information bombarded Brian. I'm sure that he realized he was in a situation where every aspect was out of his control. He could do absolutely nothing to determine the outcome of the events.

I watched as he approached the bedside, his shoulders slumped, his eyes surveyed his father's withered, yellow-tinged body. He reluctantly and soberly sobbed. He realized that he had come too late. He couldn't fix anything. He couldn't control anything. In a very short while, his father would be dead.

I walked to his side and rested my hand on his shoulder. He shrugged it away. I sensed that he was embarrassed for crying. I whispered, *"It's all right Bri-Bri."*

I craved for him to turn toward me, but he resisted. He so desperately needed comfort, yet he thwarted the solace. I believed that we had just witnessed the final barrier being drawn between my sweet son and the outer world. Brian has continued to fortify himself behind a wall of stoic avoidance toward both his family and the world in general. However, I am sure that there is still a pudgy-cheeked little boy with a bundle of energy secluded in his hard outer shell. Brian the man and Bri-Bri the child, is still a loved and treasured member of our family.

Chapter 10

Miscarried Babies

Motherhood offers the joy of nuzzling the pink, delicate cheeks and sweet, soft neck of a baby. The delicious and luscious smell of a newborn baby stimulates my brain into the visions of "Madonna and Child" encounters.

However, dark anguish has also visited my home. Becoming pregnant with two additional children and losing them both preterm, immersed the black, nefarious dagger-of-death into my delicate heart. I experienced the releasing flow of thick, red ooze from my wounded heart. I wondered, in disbelief - *why didn't the world stop – I was in pain! Can't they see that my world has changed? I lost two precious babies!*

My three-year old son seemed destined not to know the joy of siblings. We had hoped for a little brother or sister for Brian but that wish began to fade.

****

The incident began innocently enough. We were enjoying a rare weekday evening at home together when the telephone rang. It was a call from Bill's mother. The hushed conversation was brief. He hung up the phone quickly and defensively stating, *"She said that I need to meet them. She told me to come along because they don't need you. I only have to sign some papers."* Bill had completed his initial four-year military enlistment in the Air Force. Despite my misgivings, he had decided not to "re-up" for another four years. That meant that we had, of course, moved back to live next to his parents until Bill could find a career for himself. Thankfully, I had found a job with the State of Illinois. In the meantime, Bill was working at my uncle's car dealership.

Naturally, I was curious. *"What paperwork?"* I asked inquisitively.

"It's nothing. Just a form of some kind. You don't need to worry about anything," he said evasively. *"I'll just walk over to their house. Be back in a minute. You guys stay here,"* his voice being firm yet elusive.

He averted eye contact as he slunk toward the door. Bill's parents were considering some land transactions with small pieces of property that they had acquired a few years ago. Still, I didn't think this paperwork would have anything to do with that, though. Certainly, they would need me along if that were the case.

"What did your mom say to you Bill?" I asked since I had learned not to trust my in-laws.

"Nothing, really, they just me to come over quick and talk about some notes. I'll be right back." again being elusive. Instantly, I knew that there was more to the story. Whenever my mother-in-law was being secretive and mysterious, it ended up poorly for me. Before I could continue to question him, Bill hurriedly left the house for a hasty yet short walk to his parent's residence.

Everything in my spirit and mind told me to scoop up our son, Brian and follow in-step right behind him. A loud voice in my head shouted that if I did it would be the scene of a long-awaited show down between wife and mother-in-law. Every fiber in my body told me that this meeting was important, yet I couldn't make my body follow in-step behind my husband. Brian and I stayed home.

An hour later, Bill placidity entered the front door of the house. Again, evading eye contact.

"Well, what happened? What did your parents want?" I inquired anxiously. His body turned away to avert having a conversation with me.

"Tell me," I persisted. *"Tell me!"* asking again.

He took a deep breath, exhaled and quietly uttered, *"They wanted me to sign the land title papers for this house. They gave the property to me."*

Initially, I was ecstatic. Owning property would offer us some security. However, the realization of what Bill had just said became clear to me.

Obviously, my name was not on the land deed. I was not listed as an owner of the property.

I wanted to ask Bill more questions, but Bill was not in the mood for talking. Only after much urging did Bill reveal that his parents didn't want to have my name on the title. They intentionally gave the land to their son only, not to his wife, not to the mother of his child. He accepted that and signed the land title. He stubbornly defended his parents and tried to explain to me that since we were married I would automatically have legal access to the land. I didn't believe him for one second because I knew better. It was the beginning of an intense verbal argument that remained unresolved - neither of us would budge in our opinion.

This incident was a clear indication for me that Bill's true allegiance was to his parents and not to Brian and me. My opinions were confirmed as fact a few weeks later when I consulted a local attorney about the issue.

****

When I awoke, the sun was still hidden from the morning sky. Lower abdominal pain pulled me from a fitful sleep. The initial slight cramps became intense and stubborn. Running my fingers over the tender area of my lower stomach, my finger tips discovered moisture near my vagina. Looking, I discovered the blood stain on my nightgown. The second trimester had not signaled any trouble in the pregnancy. My first pregnancy had progressed without any issues so I expected an uncomplicated one this time as well. However, the issues surrounding the property ownership continued to be an intense source of stress between us as the weeks progressed. He refused to approach his parents and have my name added to the title - my insistence on the matter increased by the day.

I now knew that the absence of my name on the deed represented a bigger issue in our marriage. The increased stress built inside me. The stress increased as my pregnancy progressed. Finally, by the end of the fifth month of my pregnancy, on a most horrible day, I lost the baby.

Bill's family made no hospital visits.

"We are Memorial Hospital people not St. John's Hospital people. We don't visit people who go to the Catholic hospital," they explained cruelly. After all, a miscarried baby was not a grandchild. Bill's presence was not at my bedside.

My mother stood next to the emergency room gurney and stroked my forehead. She had experienced a similar loss and seemed to understand my pain. Still, she didn't seem to have or use the words I needed to hear. Perhaps my ears weren't hearing the words at that time. Would anyone's words help to soothe the affliction of my heart?

The emergency room personnel hustled about their duties while my body shivered my muscles cramped and the ill-fated baby was flushed from this world. The white sheets, encasing the hard gurney, were stained red. My mother stood, a silent sentinel, as the process continued. On her face was an expression of knowing and a softness of touch, which I had never experienced from her, before or since.

****

A few months passed. Unbelievably, the scene was repeated. I experienced the loss of yet another precious babe. In the emergency room again, it is as if I am participating in a predetermined plot for which there is only one ending. Sadly, the ending to this horrible scene was known before I stepped through the hospital doors. No answer was given for the loss other than providence. However, I detected little divine guidance in that situation. After a three-day hospital stay and another D & C surgical procedure, I returned to a house that still didn't belong to me and into a family which refused to accept me.

Slowly I experienced my mind, my essence, my psyche envelope within myself. It was a defense mechanism that enabled me to bear the loss of my children. Craving to stay in my grief yet hungering to be released from it, consumed me. I'm sure that the discomfort which engulfed me at this period was similar to an addict in rehab. I was irritated and agitated anticipating the next "hot shot" or snort or sniff that would soothe my ravaged world. I wanted that all- special bit of precious, god-loving, mind-enhancing, nerve-relaxing, body- releasing "hot shot" which, once received - fixed, corrected, soothed and mended their most intense and irritating life troubles. I needed that release. Every fiber in my body intensely craved that release. I searched long for that one shot that could soothe, quiet and heal my heart and console my brain but finding it was denied. Of course, the soothing is hard won. The world was raw! My body was gutted.

My inner most memories and secrets were splayed at my feet. My scarred emotions were treated like the frothy dust on the much traveled road of despair. The debris transformed the lens through which I viewed the world. My perception of blackness deepened in texture and sensation. My sullen world evolved into a tightly interwoven cocoon that excluded the outer universe.

Slowly and silently, something miraculous began to occur. The deep, inner well of strength and fortitude from within my brain began to whisper that I needed to maintain my sanity. I grasped onto tiny shreds of daily life that tethered me to reality. My heart struggled to listen to my brain. Sheer strength of will prevailed. My impassioned psyche struggled to survive. Family members with deficient insight offered little solace. They, the soft, lovable forms, went unclaimed, forever.

Nightmares containing faceless forms of babies floating into black, bottomless caverns haunted me. Reluctantly, I experienced this grotesque night time experience for many months. I was physically exhausted but dreaded the gnawing claw of sleep for I knew what the "dream" threatened to provide.

Sadly, I carry the invisible, underlying scar of battle only a mother knows - the lost campaign of struggling to save the lives of her children. Burdened with the unspoken grief, I hide the unseen sadness. My heart was no longer naïve. My brain will never forget. My soul will ever mourn!

Chapter 11

College Bound

Adult support for lifelong achievement was not offered to me in my formative years. My junior high school class was on the roster for the college entrance exam. The schedule was listed by the students' last names in alphabetical order. As each student's name was called, we were instructed to report to the principal's office to learn the time for test taking. The end of the school day arrived and all the students had been called except for me. This occurred a few weeks before the end of the school year, and I was anxious to know when I would be scheduled for the test.

Obviously, the nuns had simply forgotten to call my name. Therefore, I took the bold action of going to the office and informing the teachers of their oversight. When I confronted the principal, however, I certainly never expected her response. *"The teachers and I had a discussion about you,"* she said. *"We decided that you are not smart enough to succeed in college. Since we did not want you to be disappointed that you would fail in college, we decided not to schedule you for the entrance exams. I am sure that you can find something else to do with your life beside college. Now, I am busy. You need to go home before they lock the school doors,"* as she shifted her glance back to her paperwork.

Stinging numbness traveled throughout my body. She had mentally slapped me in the face. An adult educator had never told me outright that I was stupid. After all, I was attending a private, girls, Christian academy and getting good grades. I could not understand why the teachers would call me stupid. I don't remember leaving the office. I don't remember how

I got home. I don't remember sitting at the supper table. I do remember crying myself to sleep.

Believing that I was stupid and unable to learn at a college level shaped the next few years of my life. I graduated from high school, married, and began my life as a mother and military wife. However, there remained within me that little nagging desire that wouldn't die. It was a festering, smoldering, ember that persisted inside me. I needed and wanted something different. I enjoyed learning new things. I enjoyed reading – *"Would a dumb kid like to read?"*

I started to consider the idea that I could go back to school and study something that interested me. I wasn't sure what that would be or how I would enroll - I was scared. I remembered the words of the nuns: *"you would fail in college."* I didn't want to be embarrassed if I was indeed stupid and couldn't learn at the advanced level. Still, the idea matured and garnered strength. As I began to voice my idea, people gave me unwanted advice. They told me I should start at a community college level instead of a university. This time I was not a little girl to be dissuaded from her dreams. I would go to college, and I would do it my way. I began my journey into higher education by signing up for general education classes at Southern Baptist University in Charleston, South Carolina. My first day, I was both scared and proud. I also was fully aware that I was a mother and a wife with precious little time. The idea was now so strong within me that I knew I had to go forward. Recognizing my inner strength was empowering for me. I began classes when my youngest child was six weeks old.

At the time, my husband was on active duty in the air force and often assigned to duty in a foreign country. This meant that I frequently lived in a time crunch circle.

My husband was vaguely supportive of my return to school. He said it was good to learn new things. However, he didn't think that I would be able to graduate with a degree. The reception from both my mother and mother-in-law was less than enthusiastic. My mother-in-law was especially negative and frequently made it known that she viewed my return to academia as abandonment of my family.

Obviously, the only one in my corner was, me. I mentally struggled with this fact but finally accepted it. It was perfectly fine for me to support me. The thought gave me new strength and determination. It assisted me in my resolve. I would do my best. I would juggle the duties of mom, wife, and student. I would graduate. I realized that I only had to make all this decision once. The rest would be easier. I just needed to take each day as it came along.

Well, things surely did get rough! My three children kept growing and, of course, had school activities, gym class, after school meetings, weekend parties, doctor appointments, shopping trips for clothing, emergency room visits, library activities, shopping trips for new shoes, soft ball practice, sleepovers with friends, and all of the other activities that children engage in while growing up. In addition to all the chaos, my husband would come home from military duty on the base and announce that he was going on TDY (temporary duty) for three weeks to three months. This meant that I would be solely responsible for all family and household functions while he was away.

Developing a schedule was a necessity. I'm sure that if you would ask my children about this point in their lives, they would agree that our family life was very tightly wound. It was active, busy, non-stop, and full of adventure.

Returning to school was something that I could handle with a few adjustments to some of my preconceived notions. I discovered that it was not important that my house was military clean. It was fine to eat leftover's for dinner. The laundry didn't need to be done right away but could wait for a few loads to accumulate. Reading bedtime stories was more important than always being up-to-date on the latest news events.

I also discovered that if I packed a bag with play toys and snacks, I could take my youngest child to some of my shorter classes. Proofreading a term paper with my children while relaxing after supper gave us quality time together. I knew that I was setting a good example for my children by returning to college and getting a good education.

****

Success in one college course after another triggered anger. I got mad at myself. I was mad because I had believed the words of some old, wizen nuns at an isolated little school. I accepted it when they said that I was dumb and unable to learn. I was also mad that I hadn't listened to my inner voice sooner. I wanted so badly to return to that school in Springfield,

Illinois and scream at the teachers. I wanted to let them know that they were so very, very wrong in their assessment.

Time passed quickly, and after receiving my associate, bachelor and master degrees from prominent universities, I attended my ten-year high school reunion. There were a variety of activities planned for the reunion weekend. One of them was a choral recital in the school auditorium. I had been in the glee club and ensemble in high school. I knew that the nuns who had been in the principal's office that decisive day would be at the choral performance.

Sure enough, I saw the group of nuns huddled together, I slowly approached them. I was confident they would remember me and the incident. I introduced myself with my maiden name as I smiled and extended my right hand. When they looked at me, our eyes met. We exchanged pleasant superficial conversation about the reunion activities. Then Sister B. asked me, *"Well, Joyce how are you doing these days?"*

I delayed answering her question, I related the story of the meeting in the principal's office during my junior year. They gave me their undivided attention until I told them that I had indeed attended college and received multiple degrees. When they heard that, they averted their eyes and mumbled incoherently about not remembering the encounter. All denied the experience.

Obviously, the incident was of no consequence to the nuns. I was dumbfounded. As they began a conversation with other reunion attendees, I stepped back and fell into one of the auditorium seats with a thud. I remember sitting there silently for a few minutes as the realization become clear. Something that had been one of the pinnacles of my youth and had affected me so drastically had no significance at all for the educators involved.

While sitting there, I realized that nuns were really just people. They are no different from anyone else and do not deserve any additional respect. Simply accepting a title and putting on black clothing does not make them worthy of admiration. If a nun or priest or any other clergy person happens to be a good teacher or a competent administrator then they can earn your respect just like anyone else. The betrayal I felt from the nuns who did not seem to truly care that I had risen above their expectations was great. Their assessment contributed to the negative view I held of my self-worth.

My inability to reach my full potential early in life can be traced directly back to my ill-placed reverence for this religious community.

I had been holding on to a mythical image of nuns and priests that didn't exist. I had adopted the religious attitude of my parents without fully examining it for myself. I decided that I needed to take the pieces of religious doctrine that made sense for me and develop my own relationship to the Supreme Being. This was exciting and scary at the same time because for me it was as if the last chain of my childhood was being discarded.

****

I believed for many years that I was the first PERSON in my family to go to and graduate from college. Finishing my masters' degree offered me some free time to explore my family genealogy. As I searched, I located documents relating to my first cousin who was about five years older and had moved from our hometown shortly after high school graduation. I had interacted with him at family reunions and weekends when our fathers would visit each other, but we had grown apart. The archived documents showed that when my first cousin, John Gatschenberger, left home he moved to Hattiesburg, Mississippi. There he enrolled in Southern Mississippi University and earned a PhD. I find it extremely ironic that, as I write this chapter, I also am enrolled in a class at Southern Mississippi University in Hattiesburg, Mississippi. However, since he gained his degree before me, I had to change my claim: I am the first WOMAN in my family to go to and graduate from college. In the end, the example I set for my children was successful. They have all attended college.

Chapter 12

Erica Ann "Mud Gum" Zake

Early in my marriage I had given birth to a beautiful, healthy baby boy. I savored the joy of first-time motherhood. The ambrosia of nuzzling a newborn babe produces a lifelong loving bond. Having a child fulfils a primal drive of forming and protecting a family.

However, as we know, time moves at its own pace. Ten years later, I had been blessed with two additional children–lovely daughters. Sadly, the youngest of them was gravely ill. I had little indication of the challenging medical events that were about to shape and mold her future.

At the time, I feared that I did not have the physical strength or moral fortitude to endure the potential loss of another child. My husband, son, young daughter, and I are in a military hospital waiting room when my husband and I are called to our youngest daughter's bedside. The medical specialists' in the Intensive Care Unit (ICU) at Travis Air Force Base Hospital gave us the harrowing news: Our young, beautiful child was diagnosed with Prolific Systemic Glomular Nephritis secondary to Systemic Lupus Erythematosus. This meant that her immune system was destroying her kidneys. This medical condition also contributed to her developing a blood clotting disorder. She was dying.

I heard the doctor's talking. I saw their lips moving. I understood that they were telling me life-threatening information about my youngest child. However, my body didn't have feeling at that moment. I was not aware of whether or not the temperature in the room was cold or hot. Did the sun shine in the noon sky or was it night with the bright moon lighting the path for visitor's approaching the hospital entrance? Was it raining outside? Was the wind blowing? I couldn't answer those questions. I had an inner voice telling me that I was on overload. That is the place where a parent goes when the information he or she hears about their child is too horrible. The incoming facts were too intense in that moment: not only can I do nothing to save my child but also, I, as a parent, could do nothing to protect my child. It was a "numbness of nurturing."

I wanted so desperately to help her, yet I could only comfort her with the caring, watching attention of a concerned parent. I also needed to comfort my son and other daughter. I needed to shield them against the full punch of the awful truth concerning their baby sister. If they know the full truth about the destruction that this disease could yield, they would have run down the hall screaming in horror. At this point in time, I had been a registered nurse for twenty years. I searched for something I could do to lessen my daughter's pain and suffering. However, all I could do was sit at her bedside and hope and pray that the path we were embarking on would lead to her regaining her strength and health.

There was no Internet available for a research source. There was no established or published protocol that I could access. She was slowly fading away and the wish for her health was fading with her. She had no physical, mental, or emotional reserve left. Her skin was pale; her lips were parched, and she had only intermittent periods of lucid interactions. She had not wanted to be there, but obviously the choice was not hers to make. The disease had ravaged her body with such a brutal and pervasive force that it had robbed every bit of strength from it. She had just enough to maintain the basic functions of her tiny, fragile body. She had the staunch heart of a lion but the disease had reduced her body to a fragile, drifting feather that swayed with the changing winds. Whenever the torrid, attacking, devouring intensity of the disease would raise its ugly head, she would suffer the debilitating consequences.

Her long and torturous journey had begun when she was just ten years old. Being an active and inquisitive child offered her lots of playing opportunities. Her days were filled with playing softball with her older sister, riding her bike, skateboarding, aggravating her older brother, and competing on the community swim team.

She was a social child. Everyone who met Erica, liked Erica. Her favorite hobby was chewing different flavors of bubble gum while trying to blow the biggest bubble ever. I would look out of the kitchen window to see her blowing a bubble much bigger than her entire face. The bubble would pop, filling her face with gum residue. Quickly, she would giggle, run to the biggest mud puddle, jump in it, and dance around just to see the mud splash wildly onto the grass. That is how she got her nickname "mud, gum." It seemed to suit her. She was always a happy child, in motion.

Her life and medical status changed insidiously. However, there was one event that alerted us to it. One afternoon after school, Erica was sitting on a chair at the kitchen table with her foot elevated on a chair. Her ankle and lower leg were swollen and obviously painful. We believed that she had either injured her ankle at baseball practice or hurt it while using her skateboard. My husband took her to the emergency room at nearby Travis Air Force Base.

The medical tests did not reveal any local infections or broken bones. However, her ankle area was still painful, swollen, and warm to touch. The emergency room doctor requested a urine sample from our daughter to determine if any other infections were present in her body. Nothing was obvious. She was released with instructions to rest, hydrate, and keep her foot and ankle elevated. We applied ice packs intermittently every twenty minutes for comfort.

Surprisingly, later that evening, we received a call from the ER staff to bring our daughter back into the hospital. They informed us that her urine sample contained a much greater amount of protein than normal. Since high protein levels indicate that her kidneys were not functioning well, they needed to complete more screening tests. Within minutes of arrival, she was admitted to the ICU unit. We were told that our daughter did not have much hope of living through the night since she was in the advanced stages of kidney failure.

The specialist further explained to us that her kidney failure was caused by systemic lupus erythematosus. Her immune system saw her kidneys as if they were a foreign body and was trying to get rid of them. Complicating the situation was the fact that there was no documented or accepted medical treatment protocol for treating a child of her age with this condition. The team of medical specialists explained that any treatment they attempted would be experimental and came with no guarantees.

We were very confused how our daughter could have such a devastating disease and not shown signs of it. We hadn't noticed any medical problems with Erica. She appeared to be active and healthy.

The doctors explained to us that the decrease of her kidney functioning occurred slowly. They told us that kidneys are very resilient and able to function until their capacity is blocked entirely. When a patient is diagnosed with systemic lupus erythematosus, a large amount of scar tissue builds up in the kidney system's filtering tissue. Once the tissue is replaced by scar tissue, it can no longer filter waste material from the body and kidney failure occurs.

Within two days, Erica had changed from a happy, active social child to a medically fragile patient with very little chance of survival. We were devastated. We had no one to turn to for discussion or comfort. We had to trust our own intuition and the expertise of the doctors. We, as parents, explained to our other children what was occurring with their little sister. They didn't understand! All they could comprehend was that their little sister didn't feel well, and they would spend a lot of time either in the hospital waiting room or sitting on a chair in the ICU family lounge.

Following a few very tense days of discussion with the medical team it was decided that we would start Erica on an experimental routine of steroid pulsing and chemotherapy. The treatment would negatively affect any future bone growth and hormone development. It also would cause permanent loss of body hair. We were warned that Erica would become violently ill, experience nausea, vomiting, and weight loss. If this treatment were not attempted, Erica would die. We didn't hesitate. We signed the forms and the treatment began.

The next few months were spent either admitting or discharging Erica from the military hospital for her pulsing treatments. There were supplemented by assisting her at home to regain her strength. During that time she was home schooled. When it was obvious she was strong enough to return to a regular school setting, I went to talk with the school nurse. I needed to update her about Erica's medical condition. After a lengthy discussion, I was convinced that she understood Erica's status.

However, when I escorted Erica to her class the next day the school nurse told Erica's classmates that she had developed an immune disease. This was the time when the public was just hearing information about HIV and AIDS with Ryan White attending public school. Erica's classmates assumed that she had been diagnosed with AIDS. The school nurse did very little to clarify the issue. I spent most of that day with Erica at her school. I noted that when the parents came to pick-up their children from school, they would whisper to their child. *"Don't touch that girl. She has a bad sickness. I don't want you to get it."* Over the next few weeks Erica lost a lot of her friends.

Erica was ten years when she was diagnosed with systemic lupus erythermatosus and approaching her teen years. Most of the neighbors did not understand her illness and made little attempt to ask questions about it. She was pushed out of the in crowd at school and was no longer invited to social parties. She was shunned by most of her softball teammates. She was not welcomed back as a member of the swim team.

Our family members were supportive during this time and made a pact that Erica would always have one of us present with her for any tests or treatments. We also decided that whenever possible, we would make stressful medical situations manageable by introducing fun activities for all concerned. We learned how to make balloon animals and always made sure that plenty of coloring books and happy movies. A family member always volunteered to sleep at the hospital if Erica needed an extended hospital stay. We were all going to make this challenging medical situation as pleasant as possible. There were many days and nights when we just wanted to go home and sleep in our own beds and never look at another medical test tube again. But, if Erica couldn't go home, we wouldn't go home.

Bombarding Erica's body with harsh chemicals on a calculated schedule seemed to nudge the disease into remission for a few years. Erica continued to see an array of medical specialists and complete a battery of diagnostic tests as an outpatient- all seemed well.

****

She was fifteen years of age, and Christmas was approaching. By this time we were living in Nevada. Erica and her sister, Tarena, asked for a very special holiday gift–an airplane trip back to California to visit some close friends for a few days. Erica was doing well, medically. Tarena knew about the signs to watch for that would signal if any health issues were arising so we purchased the tickets.

The girls were so very excited. Erica was nervous just prior to the flight and said that her stomach was upset. I suggested that she ask the stewardess for some saltine crackers and a 7-up during the flight. That would help to calm her jittery stomach. The girls boarded the plane and promised to call when they arrived in California. All seemed fine!

I didn't expect the phone call from Tarena after they arrived. She told me that Erica was still not feeling well and was now vomiting and weak. I asked to talk with our friend, Sandy, who my daughters were staying with during their visit to California. My conversation confirmed my greatest fears. Erica was running a very high temperature, vomiting any food or fluids, and was weak and listless. I told Sandy to either call 9-1-1 or take Erica to the closest emergency room. She agreed and we hung up immediately so they could leave. I booked an airline passage to California.

I arrived at CW Hospital just in time to sign the consent form for Erica's emergency surgery. The surgeons removed her left kidney. The organ had stopped functioning and had died. It seems that a blood clot had formed in the vessels supplying blood to and from her kidney. This caused the kidney to die. This caused the kidney to swell and press on to the surrounding organs and tissue.

By the time the surgeons removed the swollen, necrotic kidney, it was primed to burst. The surgeons had to make a larger-than-expected incision because the area it covered was so immense. She would endure an extensive recovery process. Erica was transferred to the postoperative unit at Travis Air Force Base, and I booked Tarena an airline passage back home to Nevada.

Initially, the medical staff believed that her recovery would be uncomplicated. However, within a week she developed a staph infection and was transferred to the Intensive Care Unit. Even with careful medical monitoring, her condition continued to deteriorate. Since I had traveled from Nevada to California, the admission coordinator arranged for me to stay in an unused hospital room while Erica was cared for in the ICU. I lived out of a suitcase, and Erica lived out of an IV bag. Both of us were clinging to the fringe of life.

It was obvious that her medical condition was extremely tenuous. She would vacillate between consciousness and coma. Her fragile condition required regular blood transfusions and intravenous medication to maintain adequate circulation and aid in her recovery to general body health. In her brief periods of consciousness, we would discuss her changing medical condition and develop a plan for her discharge home to Nevada. Following a very fretful and frightful month in the intensive care unit, Erica was booked for transfer via a military medical transport to Nellis Air Force Base. I was designated as her medical chaperone. Upon arrival at Nellis, Erica was admitted to a medical-surgical unit under close observation. That was her home for the next two months. I loved my daughter so very much. You don't know how much I wished that my love was enough to make her better.

Erica had already experienced more heartache and medical challenges than most people do in a lifetime. She had missed her high school graduation, normal teenage dating, hanging out with the girls, and involvement in competitive teenage sports. I hoped that the remainder of her young life would be filled with joyous friendships, fulfillment in a career that she loved, and happy lifelong relationships. However, that was not the life program that was written for my youngest child.

The next few years were filled with doctor appointments, diagnostic tests and medication routines. Each successive year seemed to pillage and plunder a little more of Erica's body. Withstanding the everyday onslaught of the disease was an exhausting process. Sixteen years later, she was struck with the ravages of the disease again. Whenever the torrid, attacking, devouring intensity of the disease would raise its ugly head, she would suffer the debilitating consequences. This time, the site of damage was her only remaining kidney. She went into kidney failure, and a transplant was her only lifeline for survival. She had the staunch heart of a lion, but the disease progression had reduced her body to a fragile, drifting feather that seemed to sway with the changing winds. She had no reserve left. Her skin was pale and grey; her lips were parched, and she had only intermittent periods of lucid interactions.

It was the end of 2008 and Erica was enrolled in the kidney transplant program at Sunrise Hospital in Las Vegas, Nevada. Unbelievably, after she is admitted to the transplant program, the program is closed. The reason given is that there are not sufficient amount of specialized physicians in Nevada to support the program.

The entire family gathered their resources and hit the Internet to put our social network into action. We located a transplant program at the Mayo Clinic in Phoenix, Arizona. Family members were tested to determine if anyone would be suitable as a live donor. Tarena was a perfect match. She gladly agreed to give life to her sister by giving a kidney to her.

The day of surgery involved simultaneous operations for both of my daughters. This was an unexplainable situation—one which I had never previously experienced and one for which I was not prepared. The only way to sustain oneself during a situation like that was to surround oneself with caring individuals and seek medical direction from competent medical professionals. This was the case for us.

The operation was successful—a miracle occurred that day.

Total recovery for Erica took a few months. She would be under medical observation for the remainder of her life. Hopefully, it will be a very long life. Our family is so very lucky and blessed to have Erica. She adds love and attention to each and every day that would not be present in our lives without her. We are better people for having her with us. I just hope that I am deserving of Erica. She is such a wonderful gift from above!

Chapter 13

Specimen Collection

The noise crisscrossed down the hallway of the hospital corridor alerting everyone, including the nursing instructor, that something was definitely wrong. The hospital staff was already nervous since the new semester of college classes had begun, and the nursing students were starting their final rotation in the medical-surgical area. Although it would be their final semester of school, it was their first experience caring for hospitalized patients with complex medical conditions. Earlier that morning the students had paired off so that they could intensely review the conditions of select patients and prepare for any of the instructor's questions.

The students also were visibly nervous. They had taken extra time during the morning report by interrupting the night-shift nurse. As she was signing off to the day nurse, the students repeated questions concerning patients that they had pre- selected for care. The students had also bothered the maintenance staff with questions concerning use of cleaning agents and policies for disinfecting common use items. The dietary staff had reported that the students delayed the breakfast schedule by examining dishes on the patients' food cart. So, it came as no surprise when the entire medical staff heard the deafening sound of clanging bedpans and falling metal I.V. poles emitting from the unit utility room. It was obvious that nursing students caused the incident.

The nursing instructor had stationed herself at the centrally located nurses' station so she would be ready to handle any further nursing student interruptions. She was ready to respond where needed to any further casualties in the normal flow of the medical staff routine. She immediately turned to the direction of the clamor and dashed down the hall.

The two students in the utility room had been very diligent in their duties that morning. They had intentionally chosen an older, diabetic patient to care for so that they could hone their skills at collecting urine samples and interpreting glucose levels. This was before the use of glucometers to determine blood sugar levels. Specially prepared paper dipsticks were "dipped" into urine specimens to calculate the patient's current sugar levels.

The urine sample, which they had collected from the diabetic patient that morning, revealed that he had a normal glucose level. The students knew that this patient had been diagnosed as a "brittle diabetic"–meaning that his diabetic status could change often, and his condition needed to be monitored closely. They also knew that previous urine glucose checks revealed that he had a large amount of sugar in his urine. After the two students discussed the results of the test, they decided that the normal reading must be in error. They decided that they should check a urine sample from one of them since neither of them was diabetic to test the strips.

The majority of the space in the utility room was taken up by a large, deep, metal, double-sink and a few wall cabinets. Only a few patient care items and one person at a time could fit comfortably in the small, cramped space.

The more energetic of the two students' decided that she would provide the sample. However, she could not go out of the utility room to collect it. If she did, the nursing instructor would spot her and ask questions about why she was transporting patient urine samples into the community bathroom. To avoid this, she decided to stand on the sides of the large metal sink. She pulled down her panty hose and underwear, squatted, and provided the urine specimen.

As she completed this most delicate task, the other student became nervous. She felt it had been too long since the nursing instructor had checked on them. To make sure the instructor would not be appearing soon, she decided to open the door. In her haste and nervousness, she hit the edge of the large, metal sink. This, in turn, knocked the other student off of her perch and into the sink – head first. She landed with feet sticking up, encumbered by her crumpled up underwear and pantyhose. The collection cup flew up into the air and urine landed haphazardly and indiscriminately on the nursing students, the collection of metal patient care items, the cabinet doors, and the utility room walls.

The "lookout" student let out a harrowing scream which mixed with the metallic clang of the care items as they crashed to the floor. She released her grip on the utility room door, and it slammed closed with a deafening thud.

The two students froze in position. Their frightened eye contact confirmed their dreaded future. They instinctively knew that their nursing careers over. In addition, they would have an extensive clean-up job to perform. Time and space stood still.

At that moment, the nursing instructor, who had frantically raced down the hallway, flung open the door with such gusto that both nursing students shielded their faces to protect themselves from attack. This action elicited screams from not only the two students but also the nursing instructor.

It took a few moments for the instructor to assess what she was viewing. Slowly her face began to contort into a disfigurement which the students had never seen. The instructor squinted her eyes and breathlessly uttered words without moving her teeth. Without voicing a word, the students quickly began to clean up.

As the nursing instructor turned to leave, she muttered that the two students should meet her downstairs in the conference room when they had completed their task. The other nursing students whispered covertly in the hallway outside the utility room. They all wanted a final glimpse of their colleagues before they were expelled from the program.

I was the nursing student who obtained the urine specimen for the urine check. I acutely remember the situation. I was dreading the meeting but mentally prepared myself for expulsion. I had worked so very hard to reach this final semester. I had sacrificed and struggled, so I decided that no matter what the nursing instructor said, I would fight and counter negotiate.

To my delight, the instructor chose to use the experience as a learning situation. She assembled all of the nursing students who had been on the patient care floor that day. We were instructed to explain the entire situation to our peers. They listened quietly and attentively.

"What was the reading of your urine dipstick test?" one student asked after the explanation.

"My test was also normal. I didn't have a high sugar level in my urine."
"And have you learned anything from this experience?" the instructor asked.

"Well," I began, *"if I had to repeat the situation, I realize that it would have been wiser to check with the nursing instructor for guidance before doing my own investigation and inventing new testing procedures."* My co-conspirator had no comment.

At this point, the instructor began a brief lecture and pointed out the issues of patient confidentiality and student safety. She taught us how to check the expiration date on the bottle of urine dipsticks and how to track the last 24 hours of patient urine glucose readings.

This situation was just one of many interesting experiences that I either created or encountered during my nursing education years. The variety of life incidents that occurred for my family and me during these years were certainly life changing. In addition to nursing episodes, our military family relocated multiple times, providing non-traditional learning experiences. During each new military assignment, we would absorb the local cultural values of each geographic area in which we lived. Our family absorbed the good bits of social values from each community in which we were relocated. These bits became part of our family culture and made it much easier to assimilate into each new community.

I entitled this chapter "Specimen Collection," because in addition to the stories of my nursing exploits, I have added other stories from that time in my life. The memories of the different cultures we were exposed to during this period are also specimens we collected. The friends and friendships were other specimens from this part of my life.

****

I entered college at the age of twenty-seven when I had three small children to tend. My husband was a full-time, active duty United States Air Force career sergeant involved in worldwide search and rescue missions. This assignment required frequent home absences. Because my college courses also required time away from home, my children often accompanied me to most of my classes. I started the morning by helping my children to dress and filling up their backpacks with snacks and playtime toys. These articles would distract and entertain them during my college classes. In that way, my children went to college before they entered kindergarten. However, the schedule got much more difficult to balance when they entered grade school. It seemed that each of us was always either going to an activity or coming from one. This required a strict schedule to maintain an orderly family routine. It got to the point that I had to write out our weekly routine on paper in increments and make sure that everyone had a copy. Often, when my husband was home from a military mission, we would meet each other in the driveway for only a few moments to exchange household information while greeting each other. My class homework was often completed while I was reading a good night story to my children at bedtime.

When I began to work, I chose the evening shift at the hospital (3:00p.m.– 11:00p.m.). Because my husband worked during the day at the military base, someone was always available to care for our children. The only difficult this caused was when we wanted to spend time with each other. Frequently, we would cut our schedules painfully close. It was even more difficult to arrange a date night for ourselves.

Our children grew up understanding that their parents were trying to achieve a better lifestyle for them. They were able to see the sacrifices that needed to be made to achieve that goal. Even with that view in mind, I am sure that we could have benefited from more quality time together and more opportunities to interact closely as a family.

Military life, with its frequent relocations, offered our children many opportunities to meet new classmates and discover new geographic areas that they would otherwise not have been able to visit. Some of these relationships have continued into their adulthood.

****

My college and nursing career progressed to the point where I had completed my associate, bachelor, and master degrees. I was finally able to start my nursing career and direct more attention to my children's activities. At this point, the children were in their teenage years and testing the lines and rules of social behavior. My husband was also reaching the point in his military career where he was considering retirement from military service.

By this point, the difference in our worldview became very noticeable when we would make trips back to our hometown. Others in our extended families or old neighborhoods that had not experienced anything outside of their home communities did not have the specimens we had gathered. Their base of knowledge about the rest of the world was extremely limited. These people didn't know how other people in other neighborhoods operated or how others viewed the world. To us, the views and opinions of the world were so much broader and tolerant than those held by our family members. Upon returning home, we found that family members seemed prejudice and small-minded. They were also more guarded with their opinions concerning issues of politics, religion, and other human relations.

Prior to our travels, I hadn't noticed this difference between us and our extended family members. Afterward, it was glaringly evident. It quickly escalated an issue between us and our extended family. The longer our visits lasted, the more our opposing views and the discussions they generated were pushing us psychologically apart. It only took a couple of years for our family to view the world very differently than our extended family. As time went on, our extended family began to see us as radicals who held wild ideas. It became more difficult for us to even consider planning visits to our extended family.

The only exception to this trend in our family was my husband's attitude. Although he was exposed to the same culturally diverse neighborhoods as the rest of us and had seen the variety of methods available to solve issues and problems, he was not solid in his beliefs. I thought that he was developing a broader view of the world just as we were. During our private family interactions, he would agree with us and express an accepting attitude toward new ideas. However, when we would visit his family, he would re-adopt their compacted attitudes and views. This made the visits home even more confusing and problematic. It was like he had two different personas—one of a well-traveled family man who supported his ever changing family's needs and experiences and the other of an inter-dependent little boy who looked to his parents to provide him with his views and direction.

This wavering added strain to our marriage. Whenever we were around his extended family, he would verbally downgrade my opinions or statements. His mother always seemed to be on the opposite side of my statements, and he would always state that her opinion was the best one in each and every matter. Even if his mother was not present, he would support his older, twin sisters. Sometimes, I wanted him to plan family activities with his children and me while we were visiting. Instead, he would involve his mother and sisters. In the end, they would plan our weekend schedule.

The strain became so great that, by the end of his life, he physically separated himself from our family. At the time, he had retired from the military. Instead of physically filing for divorce or approaching me with a direct conversation about his feelings, he accepted a job in Ohio working for an associate in the insurance business. He also rented a small, private apartment in Reno, NV. In retrospect, this physical absence from our family helped him to psychologically abandon us. Sadly, his distance allowed him to informally divorce me - in his mind, at least. This was very evident to me as I was organizing the papers in his briefcase after his death.

In it, I discovered a sensual love letter, intimate love making items, and bank statements for an account I was unaware existed. He concealed it by sending the account statements to his older sister, Lu, in Illinois. He also had used the account to finance his covert life with his latest girlfriend, one of many throughout his lifetime. He hadn't, however, designated a beneficiary for this account.

Bill's extended family was well aware of this account and his secret activities during his life. When our son Brian asked about the account after his death, his sister Su answered, *"I just thought that it was part of the estate."* Well, if my husband had an estate, I can assure you that neither I nor his children had knowledge of its existence.

I guess that I should have noticed the gradual disappearance from his psychological attachment to our family, but I was so ultimately trusting that I was caught totally unaware. Obviously, these new specimens of ardor revealed that our marital union had been built on lies and dishonesty—at least by the end of our relationship. It was then painfully obvious to me that our marriage had been in trouble and I didn't realize it.

I now wonder deep in my soul if I suspected his unfaithfulness but chose to ignore it. Did I consciously turn my head when I noticed that the signs? I know other women in this situation seem to ignore the obvious. Was I one of them? I ask myself these questions repeatedly. Possibly, I was scared that our union would not hold up under examination. Could it be that I was afraid of approaching the dissolution of our marriage? I trusted him so totally and loved him so fully that the fact that he did not return and share those feelings for me never occurred to me. Yes, I was naïve in that regard. I will never be caught emotionally off-guard again – I have learned to openly discuss my feelings. I will be more diligent about specimen collection in the future. All the little pieces of information in my life are important and they fit together to make a bigger picture and tell a story – give a diagnosis.

I have learned through this process that I am vulnerable. I was lured into believing that love was forever and self-sustaining. Still, I have not given up on love. I can give my heart and soul to another person for safekeeping. I continue to believe that the right person will hold it forever in a safe and trusted place. Somehow, even after surviving such a devastating betrayal, some of my trust and openness to vulnerability remain intact. I am still a human being capable of connecting with other humans and able to share feeling of love and compassion.

So after collecting all the specimens from my life with Bill and looking at the pieces with as much objectivity as a wounded woman can muster, I realize that I was only a very small strand of Bill's life. Believing that he and I could form a strong, loving family was my weak line in the whole DNA chain of our marriage.

The diagnosis seems to be that Bill couldn't be truthful to me or his children because he couldn't be true to himself.

Chapter 14

"Ant Lan"

This is a week for two anniversary celebrations. My three sisters, one brother and I have all gathered for our youngest sister's wedding in a rustic cabin in North Carolina. My sister Leann, five years my junior, reminds me that this also is the date of her 40th wedding anniversary. I stop making table decorations, a breath catches in my throat, and I turn toward her.

"Unbelievable! I can't imagine that I forgot your anniversary," I say. My memory quickly races back forty years to St. Agnes Church.

****

It's a hot, muggy August day in 1973. I'm dressed in a floor length, pink, floral gown and following my similarly dressed older sister down the church's main aisle. I approach the nervous groom and groomsmen standing with the priest at the base of the altar. Tom will soon marry my younger sister, Leann.

My three-year old son, Brian, is the ring bearer. I have just been discharged from the hospital after experiencing my second miscarriage. I am emotionally and physically fragile. I have not had time to process the stirring sentiments of the loss of yet another child. The activity-filled week has been focused on wedding preparations.

I approach the altar, take my appointed place and watch my sister Leann as she and her finance, Tom, profess their marriage vows. I wonder if their life together will follow a similar, predictable path to mine: marriage and family life in the same town in which they were born and raised.

When my husband completed his initial four years of United States Air Force enlistment and decided not to reenlist, we transported our belongings via U-Haul back to our childhood residence in Springfield. We were still unsure of our lives' direction. We had retreated back to the security of our extended family environment to determine our own family path. Our world seemed unsettled. Of course, my husband had the big dream of being successful in business but had not developed a plan to achieve his goal. We settled into a small, rented house in a rural town. My husband had taken a job that offered no option for advancement at an auto dealership operated by my uncle. I initially accepted the roll of housewife.

My thoughts momentarily drift back a few years to our childhood in which Leann and I shared a family life that was both stressful and filled with secrets. Leann is five years' my junior and carries a different personality. I constantly wanted to leave home, see the world, have wonderful experiences, ask questions, see how things operate, and determine how parts fit together. Sweet Leann had quietly watched and learned to be content, to be quiet. She was not a child who would be noticed in a group, but she was observant. I can understand this. She grew up in a home where it was much more beneficial to be quiet, invisible, and hidden.

It was so much better to be quiet and invisible in our home in order to increase your chances of avoiding intense harm. Leann obviously learned this lesson better and sooner than I had. Her intelligent mind was not given to asking inquisitive questions or being involved in our childhood investigative exploits. Often, she would quietly observe situations and conclude the answer for herself. She avoided trouble by not questioning our parents and not expecting any attention. When we grew older and gathered for family functions, we would talk about our childhood.

"I just tried to be invisible," she would say.

Leann was such a beautiful child and is such an accomplished adult. It is a shame she had to practice being so inconspicuous as a child. I often look at family pictures and focus on Leann's cute, little face and bright smile. I realize that she is standing in the background and rarely posing for attention. However, I do note that she assumed a posture of protection for our younger brother, Chuck. It is obvious that she realized at a young age that he was also the object of physical and verbal abuse from both of our parents.

When my young granddaughter, Kiyah, was learning to say a few choice words she attempted to say *"Aunt Leann."* It was a difficult exercise for her. She tried and tried unsuccessfully. Some individual syllables were a challenge. However, she did manage to pronounce *"Ant Lan."* This notation has become a family term of endearment referring to my sister. We all enjoy a little chuckle as we repeat it and give my sister Leann a hug. To this day, when I see my sister I extend my arms and give her a big hug and repeatedly say in a loving voice *"Ant Lan, Ant Lan."*

Leann earned her nursing degree while raising her four children. She had always maintained a hectic daily agenda while balancing her work schedule and fulfilling her parenting duties. Additionally, she always volunteered for school socials and family functions when needed. This was especially true when my husband of thirty-five years was diagnosed with terminal cancer.

Leann's generosity was also evident when my youngest daughter needed a kidney transplant. We were living in Las Vegas, Nevada and needed to travel to the Mayo clinic in Phoenix, Arizona. Since my older daughter would be the donor and my youngest daughter would be receiving her older sister's kidney, each of my daughters needed a caregiver during the procedure. I cared for my younger daughter, and Leann gladly agreed to care for my older daughter during the entire ordeal.

My sister secured a leave from her job, traveled to Nevada, and then accompanied us to Arizona. We all resided in hotel-like living quarters for a few months sharing kitchen facilities and general living quarters with other transplant families. Leann was indispensable in not only assisting my older daughter before and after surgery but in providing psychological support for me as well. I had the unique situation of having both of my daughters in the operating room at the same time. Each was undergoing major surgery. Leann's support was invaluable.

****

Bill was diagnosed with cancer that was categorized as a soft tissue sarcoma. This type of cancer is usually caused by exposure to Agent Orange - Bill was repeatedly exposed to during his active duty military service. When the medical diagnosis was confirmed Bill became belligerent and defiant. He was combative with the doctor during medical visits: yelling, cussing, and screaming. The prognosis was poor and the long-term outlook for his survival was extremely low. Bill had no intention of accepting this calmly.

The doctors explained all treatment options including side effects and let Bill make the treatment decision. Bill and I discussed his options, and he decided to try experimental chemotherapy in order to reduce the size of tumor and growth rate of the cancer. Every resource indicated that survival beyond a couple of months was extremely doubtful - that it was a death sentence for my marriage partner.

Armed with this information my husband and I decided to make the best effort for a cure with whatever technology available. After completing a series of chemotherapy infusions with his local doctor and consulting with a local cancer specialist, we contacted the medical staff at M.D. Anderson Medical Center in Texas for additional evaluations. We selected this medical facility after doing extensive research by questioning medical providers and finding computer reviews. Everything indicated that this institution was the best treatment center.

The specialist at the Texas clinic reviewed the medical information available for my husband and completed additional blood analyses and body imaging tests. Their final evaluation matched the opinion of our local physicians—even with intense chemotherapy, my husband had only a few months to live.

The team of specialists developed a plan of care and we returned home to continue treatment with his initial cancer care team. My husband refused to accept this final medical decision and became belligerent toward any intervention I suggested. He became an angry, aggressive, combative, secretive recluse. He refused to discuss his feelings or fears. When I would ask if he wanted to eat or have his favorite drink, he would turn his head to the side, squint his eyes, make a snarling noise and purse his lips to create a hissing sound. I sensed that Bill desperately wanted to reveal some secret that he had kept hidden for a very long time. However, he was experiencing an internal struggle that was draining any remaining psychological strength that remained. He soon quit talking to me at all.

One day, he came out of the bedroom after secretly talking to someone on the telephone and announced that he was going back to M.D. Anderson Medical Center to get another medical opinion. He announced that this time his sister Su was going to accompany him.

Just as he finished telling me his unbelievable news, the phone rang. I answered. It was Su. She said, with a spiteful tone to her voice: *"I'm going to make a trip to Texas with your husband. Gee, are you surprised? Don't you ever talk to your husband, Joyce?"*

My response was fleeting. Knowing that the professionals had informed Bill of his condition I couldn't understand what new therapy had been discovered in the past few weeks. Bill snatched the phone from my hand and walk into another room to continue his conversation with his sister, privately.

In order to maintain medical insurance coverage for Bill's care, which was provided by my employment, I needed to continue working. I had already used every possible day off to help Bill with medical appointments and care issues. I had also borrowed sick days from gracious fellow employees who offered their sick days for my use. I had even taken days without pay and was in danger of losing my job if I spent any more time away from work. I was acutely aware that if I didn't have medical insurance for Bill's care, he wouldn't be able to get treatments that eased his pain and helped him in his cancer struggle. The medical coverage offered by the Veterans Administration did not cover the intensive care that Bill needed to adequately treat his aggressive form of cancer.

Bill didn't care about my logical assessment of the situation. Bill didn't listen. Su's had decided that I didn't want to help my husband and that it was now her duty to cure her brother.

They went to M. D. Anderson. They got the same results. They returned to our home. I imagine she had decided that it was her duty to see to his every need. We now had an uninvited house guest. She was not flummoxed. She was determined.

This unpopular invasion at such a vulnerable time made me wonder if he brought his personal guard. She provided assurance that as his body began to fail him he wouldn't reveal guarded secret.

Household decisions and routines usually were a family process but this was now past history. Sitting quietly at my husband's bedside and softly holding his parched hand was interrupted by our house guest.

When my children and granddaughter wanted to have their personal, quiet time to say their goodbyes, their islands of solitude were denied.

Daily phone calls were made to extended family in the form of a progress report.

The situation became more intense as my husband's death neared.

Additional intrusive family members arrived just as the hospice nurse was adding the morphine drip to Bill's medication.

The triad of the uninvited clan left our home only when Bill couldn't verbally or physically respond. It was as if they had assured that whatever long held secret Bill had guarded would accompany him to his grave – leaving a trail of uncomfortable memories and regrettable situations to lay rancid in our family's heritage.

****

"Ant Lan" graciously answered my pleading request and offered non-intrusive nursing assistance to our family as my husband was in his final days of life. She helped not only with hospital bedside care but comforting home-based care as well.

Leann and I together were able to approach my husband's needed care in a proven, united, caring and scientific front. We provided a strong nursing approach. This coalesced strategy physically and emotionally prevented the intrusive clan from completely imprinting totally negative memories of my husband's final days into my children's lives.

Leann's generosity was again evident when my youngest daughter, who had been diagnosed with Systemic Lupus, needed a kidney transplant. We were living in Las Vegas, Nevada and needed to travel to the Mayo clinic in Phoenix, Arizona. We stayed at the clinic for a few months for the initial testing, transplant and follow-up evaluation. My older daughter would be the donor and my youngest daughter would be receiving her older sister's kidney. This required that each of my daughters have a care giver during the procedure. I was the care giver for my younger daughter and Leann, gladly agreed to escort my older daughter during the entire transplant ordeal. My sister secured a leave from her job and traveled to

Nevada and then accompanies us to Arizona. We all resided in "hotel-like" living quarters for a few months sharing kitchen facilities and general living quarters with other transplant families. Leann was indispensable in not only assisting my older daughter before and after surgery but in providing psychological support for me as well. I had the unique situation of having both of my daughters in the operating room at the same time. Each was undergoing major surgery. Leann's support was invaluable.

****

"Ant Lan's" role as a caregiver for my family has been a long and complicated one. She was the main caregiver for our mother when she became frail and infirm later in life. This was not an easy task since our mother suffered from a variety of chronic medical conditions that required intense monitoring. Our mother was resistant to medical routines that would ease her discomfort. Therefore, she would constantly notify Leann that things needed to be changed or adjusted to meet her needs.

Leann was attentive and responsive but our mother was a difficult patient. I admire my sister's patience and persistence. Leann was also at our mother's bedside in the hospice program when she passed away. I traveled from Nevada to Illinois when it was obvious that our mother had a short time left in her life. I arrived at her bedside minutes after her passing. Leann again held and steered the ship for our family while she alone sat at our mother's bedside, helped her to take her final breath, and helped her view her final glance at life.

Leann had additional medical issues to deal with when her husband of many years was diagnosed with Parkinson's disease. This chronic, progressive, neurological disease which appears chiefly later in life is marked with tremors, weakness of resting muscles, and a shuffling gait. This condition required that her husband take medication to manage the symptoms of the disease. He had negative side effects from the medication. Obviously, he could not continue employment. Leann became the chief breadwinner for the family. This placed a financial burden on them.

Even though Leann and I live miles apart, we keep in contact with each other on a regular basis. Our regular phone calls provide a pathway for information exchange concerning family activities, professional advances in nursing and current opinions on regional and local government activities. I always value her opinions and viewpoints.

Leann has been married for forty years, raised four beautiful, college educated children, and practiced as a competent registered nurse for many years. In my eyes she is a survivor, a protector, a mentor and a wonderful member of our family. She is my younger sister but she has an "old" soul and loving heart. When I say "Ant Lan" I say it with love.

****

Where Leann has a healthy, sibling relationship with me, I cannot fail to contrast it with the intrusive clans unhealthy one with their brother. I reminisce about my father's sisters and their overly vigilant attitude toward him after he grew to manhood.

Only after long hours of deliberation was I able to consider the possibility that I had put myself and my children into a similar situation. Had I unknowingly married a man who couldn't separate from his childhood family when he grew to manhood? Had I repeated a dysfunctional pattern? Oh, horrors of horrors, had I married a man like my father?

On closer reflection, I realized that my own father demonstrated the same tendencies as my husband. My father wasn't available to my mom, my siblings, or me. Instead, he relied on his older sisters for direction when making life-changing decisions. My father would get into the car and drive to "The Sisters Three" whenever he was trying to make an important decision.

My husband was also not available in similar ways. This unhealthy interdependence that existed between my husband and his sisters extended far beyond childhood. It created a condition of abulia and a struggle making decisions for my husband. I didn't see, or more importantly understand, the pattern until I had endured and examined thirty-five years of a one-sided marriage.

Chapter 15

Queen of the World – Goddess of All

From the start she was special,
Easy to see-
She was not going to fit into any preset mold.
This was evident by the time she was a year old.

We went to the sea to gather some stones,
She gathered a lot, couldn't take them all.
She would have to choose.
Only take the "special" ones;
Let the other ones fall.

She was the leader -
But not always the lead.
She was curious enough
Yet smart to check the advice she must heed.

Danger was seductive,
Yet she pretended not to care.
When questioned by authority,
She would act like a bear!

She explored and questioned;
She tried, and she fell.
The greatness would come
But not until she climbed out of the deep, dark well.

The answer came in the most *unlikely way.*
Her own sweet BABE that was born,
Brought a wonderful new day-
She had found her path; she had found her way.

Tarena was the second of three children. She wore the role or big sister with bluster and fortitude. No one told her about gravity or the word "can't." She took one look at the world and decided that it was made for her to enjoy. Her blond hair, light skin, and brown almond eyes made an impression on everyone who encountered her. Once she set her mind to a task it was done. Her great-grandmother, grandmother, and mother had passed her the double-edged sword of stubbornness and curiosity. All she had to do was decide how to wield it to her advantage: That task would take her a lifetime.

Tarena's own birth position was breech. She came out butt first and screaming. She forewarned the world that she was here and it needed to get ready. It gave her joy to look into every nook and cranny of her world and discover what made it tick.

Sleep or naps were not something that helped Tarena through this process. She accepted them only after sheer exhaustion. Most babies and young children sleep hours a night in addition to a daytime nap. This foolishness was not for Tarena even as a young child. Her nighttime sleep pattern was short but sweet, at least for her parents.

Awaking first was always in the morning was always her goal. Usually early morning darkness filled the house along with Tarena's activity. As a concerned parent, I took her to our family doctor to make sure that she was physically healthy and growing according to her age. Sure enough, she was right on target.

She was a healthy child with a very healthy quest for life. She was going to investigate every aspect of it until she understood what made her world go "tick-tock." We, as parents, always had to make extra special adjustments to address safety issues and guard against her constant inquisitive adventures. She was always quick to disarm any child safety instrument we put in her way.

Since Tarena was awake in the pre-dawn hours, she imagined that everyone in the home should also be awake. She would enter her brother's bedroom and talk to him. When he didn't wake up, she would stick the tip of her slobbery, wet fingers in his eye and say loudly *"Eyeeeee."* Then, she progressed to his nose and repeated *"Nosessss"* followed by *"Earrrrrr."*

Well, you can image this would wake him. Then they would argue: Her brother wanted to sleep; Tarena wanted to play. When Tarena's efforts failed to produce the intended results with her brother, she would come to our room and repeat the process. I expected to awake very early most mornings with the ole' slobbery, wet poke in the face routine., accompanied by the soft, sweet alluring voice of my own dear child saying: *"mommy's eyeeeee"* etc.

After trying several remedies to avert the unwanted pre-dawn wake-up calls, I stumbled onto a solution. I cleaned out the bottom shelf of a kitchen cabinet and a section of the lower shelf of the refrigerator. In the cabinet, I put a variety of small, multi-colored plastic bowls, cups, spoons, and plates. Next to these were child- sized boxes of dry cereal and raisins. The shelf in the refrigerator held small, pre- filled containers of milk, water, juice, and cut-up fruit. I told Tarena that if she woke early in the morning, she could fix her own breakfast. The next evening, we all went to sleep. I held my breath and waited.

In the morning, I was amazed when the alarm clock woke me and the sun was shining into the bedroom. I had slept through the night. I froze for a moment in my nice warm bed and listened. I heard the faint sound of a child singing. The melody was coming from the kitchen. Joy filled my heart when I saw my sweet Tarena sitting at her small child's table, singing, and eating her breakfast. She had filled her early morning hours with her own private party. We had all enjoyed a good night's sleep.

****

Tarena was filled with curiosity and intellect. She gobbled up information like kids eating cotton candy at the county fair. This combination meant that she was quick to assess situations, inhaling the knowledge and forming her opinion about the details. When she entered school, the subjects of science and math intrigued her. She entered book reading and poetry writing contests at the local library. Her teachers always gave a good report during parent/teacher conferences. Her school science fair entries usually garnered high honors.

However, community and school events operated on certain defined guidelines. These strict regulations often appeared restrictive to her. When she felt limited, Tarena would rebel against whatever or whomever it was that was placing any constraints on her.

Tarena also always enjoyed testing the rules. One afternoon, Tarena's rebellious personality quirks converged into one statement. It initially seemed to be innocent, but it was a prophetic gateway into a change for her lifestyle and our family dynamics.

Tarena and I were walking back to the car from one of the science fairs. She had just won another first place award.

"Mom, I am not going to be smart anymore," she said, shocking me a bit.

"Why would you say that? You just received an award for your project," I replied.

"Because kids don't like you if you're smart," she said with conviction.

I should have spent more time talking with her at this point because after this interaction her focus in school and friends changed. The shift was subtle at first, but gradually, Tarena's personality and attitude changed completely.

Tarena's ability to distort the truth about her activities was glorious and shocking. She could look me in the eye, keep her calm composure, and tell an untruth as though she were in the Catholic Church confessional booth. Looking into her eyes, I desperately wanted to believe her responses, yet my "child lying" thermometer was blinking red. Middle school gave her the arena to enjoy the hormone surge of preadolescence, but she had no desire to control the new array of opportunities that the world offered to such a ripe, sensual being. She figuratively and literally jumped in with both feet. She inherited her father's addictive personality and always wanted to find the illusive, wonderful, awe-inspiring, glorious feeling that comes with the use of artificial chemicals.

The last years of and few years after high school for her were gobbled up and wasted with periodic illegal drug use. She thought that she would throw added charges of petty larceny as well. Try as I would, I couldn't determine where she was living or who her friends were. I thought that there was a small glimmer of hope when I helped her secure a job at the student health center at the University of Nevada at Las Vegas where I was employed. She received a discount on classes since I was a nurse at the university health center. I assisted her in getting funds from a government grant for the rest.

Unfortunately, she used the grant money to buy more drugs. She also was making drug contacts through the clinic clerk who worked in the front office. This clerk helped get me suspended from my nursing position at the clinic. When the bill came due for her college classes, Tarena had no money left, so I paid the balance.

It seemed that she was spiraling furthering and furthering down the black hole of drug use and association with unsavory friends. We would receive the proverbial 2:00 a.m. collect phone calls from the Detention Center. She would cry and yell into the phone telling us that the jail was dirty. She complained that she didn't have any toilet paper when she went to the bathroom in front of everyone else.

Hearing that your sweet child is sitting in jail on concrete benches next to street-wise hookers minus their underwear will give any parent visions of horror. We would accompany Tarena to meetings with court appointed lawyers who gave no assurance of legal relief. Talking to your teen-aged daughter though state office buildings that have glass partitions smeared with snot, spit, and vomit certainly is not the way a parents wants to spend a weekend.

Unfortunately, this lifestyle occupied most of Tarena's early 20's. She had not completed college classes and was in a downward spiral of employment at low- paying, menial jobs. Her future appeared very bleak and lost. Even with all of our love, caring, and support there seemed to be no positive door for Tarena to open and walk through. No matter how much a parent loves his or her child, sometimes there is nothing that can be done for the child. Watching your child slowly kill herself is gut wrenching. Tarena seemed to not care about even looking for a door of opportunity much less walking through it.

I know that you have heard this before, but just when you thought that things couldn't get any worse, things did. Tarena became pregnant.

There didn't seem to be any plans for marriage. She was going to be a single parent and wasn't able to take care of herself much less a small child. My baby was having a baby. She was living in a girlfriend's spare bedroom and working at a fast-food restaurant during the second trimester of her pregnancy. I knew that if she delivered a drug addicted baby that it would probably end up in the social services system. I had not envisioned my grandchild growing up in foster care.

My husband and I reviewed our options and then made the big decision: we kidnapped our daughter. Unannounced, we went to our daughter's friends' home and told Tarena that we were taking her out to dinner. We put her into our car and drove back to our home- a small house with few amenities on an unpaved road on the outskirts of a small town outside of Las Vegas. If Tarena was going to get access to any of her close circle of friends or mind enhancing chemicals, she was going to have to walk miles and over mountains in the hot sun. She was not inclined to do so.

She stayed with us for the remainder of her pregnancy. Initially, under extreme resistance but then, as her mind cleared of the drugs, she grudgingly agreed. The pregnancy first appeared to be just another challenge for Tarena to overcome but as it progressed just the reverse seemed to be the case.

Tarena prepared for motherhood like high school seniors eagerly preparing for a graduation ceremony. She mentally and physically morphed into the queen of expectant mothers. She read books and pamphlets on babies, anatomy changes, and motherhood. Shopping at baby boutiques, searching for the latest styles in baby clothes kept her busy. She kept each and every doctor's appointment to assess the growth and development of her baby. She reconnected with her clean circle of high school friends who were also becoming new parents. It was obvious that being pregnant was changing her life. However, our entire family was involved. Her brother was going to be an uncle. Her sister was going to be an aunt. Oh, joy, we were going to be grandparents.

Birth was approaching. Our lovely, drug-free daughter was returning to her former self and now was familiar to us. Before our eyes she was changing into an expectant mother. We assisted Tarena to preregister for birth at Sunrise Hospital and made reservations at a hotel next to the hospital. We planned to be available to assist with the delivery process when needed. We were still anxious about the physical condition of the baby, since it had been exposed to an illicit chemical environment in the early trimester of her pregnancy. Time seemed to tick off slowly yet whiz quickly in the wind. It was a very confusing yet wonderful time. We completed the hospital preregistration process.

The day approached. We checked Tarena into the birthing suite. She stated that she felt comfortable and relaxed. Initially, the labor progressed as expected. She insisted that we return to the hotel for the evening. We complied. I have experienced five pregnancies myself. I knew that her labor would progress throughout the evening and by early morning she would be ready for delivery. Since this was her first pregnancy and she was a strong willed individual, she firmly disagreed with my opinion. She stated several times that she didn't want the family to return to the hospital until late morning the next day.

I knew that if we delayed our return, we would enter into a hectic delivery room only to be greeted by a vocal and demanding daughter in the last stages of active labor. Family members made several phone calls to the birthing center throughout the night to assess her progress. This was a time in the electronic world before cell phones, laptops, or instant messaging. We were all at the mercy of a landline telephone.

Sure enough, when we enter the delivery suite the next morning, we find our daughter in the last stage of active labor. She was experiencing the intense feeling to push–a sure sign that the birth of the baby was imminent. The obstetrician was present, and the pediatrician was on call for the delivery. We supported our daughter during the last phase of the delivery process and enjoyed the first sight of our brand new granddaughter. She was born at 8:05 a.m. June 3rd, 2000, in obvious perfect health. Even though she was covered with shiny, white vernix, body fluids, and blood, the first time that I laid my eyes on my granddaughter, I knew that she was my "little bit" of heaven. A beautiful, sweet, healthy, gorgeous baby girl joined or family on that day.

Soon after her birth, complications arose. My daughter's vaginal bleeding increased instead of decreasing and can't be stopped. There is a danger of death due to hemorrhaging. Fortunately, the doctor is diligent with intervening life-saving procedures.

The maternity staff physically shifted their actions into high gear, signaling the danger. The pediatrician nimbly accepted my granddaughter in a waiting, warmed blanket, and she was taken to the newborn nursery. The obstetrician determined that the afterbirth, a collection of maternal tissue that surrounds, protects, and feeds the baby during the pregnancy, had not been expelled from my daughter's uterus.

Normally, muscle contractions of the mother's uterus occur after the baby is born. This causes the blood vessels within this tissue close off, and the tissue to be expelled from the uterus. In my daughters' situation, this process did not occur, posing a real danger of death.

I overheard the obstetrician as she quietly whispers to the delivery staff that the vaginal tissue had grown into my daughter's uterus lining and was continuing to bleed. She quickly and expertly changed into sterile exam gloves to remove the tissue manually.

I slowly and quietly moved to the head of the bed to touch my daughter's hand and sooth her vocal concerns which pierce the heavy, pregnant quiet in the room. Suddenly, our daughter's facial color drastically changed from fleshy pink to granite white. I was horrified witnessing the speed of the change in her skin color.

While frantically busy dislodging retained uterine tissue from my daughter's uterus, the obstetrician ordered two units of blood for a transfusion, which the delivery room nurses administer within a few minutes. The obstetrician slowly announced to the delivery room staff that my daughter's uterus was responding and clamping down. The healthy, fleshy pink color returned to my daughter's face, and her rate of breathing slowed to a normal rhythm. Her previously weak yet shrill voice regained some of its relaxed tone, and she softly asked to see and hold her newborn daughter.

The delivery room nurse positioned my newborn granddaughter next to my daughter's cheek for their first flesh-to-flesh touch and eye-to-eye contact. My granddaughter's tiny, fragile fingers slowly gripped my daughter's outstretched finger. My daughter nuzzled her daughter's neck and inhaled her fresh, newborn smell. I had a strong sense that this newly forming bond would last a lifetime.

Knowing that my daughter was medically stable and in competent hands, I kissed her, hugged her shoulders, and told her that I was going to accompany the pediatrician to the nursery for an examination of her beautiful daughter. On hearing this, she asked me to give her a list from her bag. It contained possible spellings she compiled for her daughter's name.

Since I was a registered nurse with a license to practice in Nevada, the pediatrician requested that I assist him while he conducted his initial newborn exam of my granddaughter. What a joy it was for me! I'm huddling in the newborn nursery next to the doctor in front of the isolette containing my precious, lovely granddaughter, and it was exhilarating.

We both examined the pink, pudgy, healthy, newborn miracle. I assisted the doctor in measuring her head and length. I cuddled her soft, supple, pink body as the exam continued. During the exam, the doctor placed my daughter's list of potential names for my granddaughter, on the mat of the isolette so that he could look at them while examining the baby. He slowly repeated each name, stating that he wanted to make sure that the name matched the personality of the child.

"I like the spelling and the name K-I-Y-A-H the best," he finally says. We completed the newborn exam, and I returned to the delivery suite to check on my daughter.

With the passing of a few hours, my daughter's condition was medically stable, and she was experiencing some well-earned moments of rest. She was weak and drowsy but healthy. She slowly opened her eyes when I entered the birthing suite. She inquired about the choice of names from the pediatrician. I related that he chose the spelling of K-I-Y-A-H. She sleepily agreed. The birth certificate was completed. After a couple days, my daughter and granddaughter were medically cleared and released. We all traveled home to Pahrump, Nevada.

A few months later, my daughter secured a job and was able to move into her own apartment. She was now a competent, loving single mom raising her child within the circle of a loving, extended family.

****

Tarena has been and is a great, nurturing single mother. She completed her college studies and obtained a master's degree in curriculum development. She became a good example for her daughter in regards to her lifestyle and moral development. Having a baby literally saved Tarena's life.

In her transformation, Tarena gave birth to more than just a healthy, sweet child. She also gave her younger sister a new lease on life. When it became apparent that her sister was at death's door, Tarena offered the gift of life. Due to complications from Systemic Lupus, her younger sister needed a new kidney. Tarena gladly stepped up to be tested for compatibility. She was found to be a 99% match: something rarely found in donor matching. She gladly gave her sister a kidney and literally saved her life.

It has been a long and complicated road for Tarena since she started as a little girl sitting in the dark kitchen singing and eating her breakfast from little plastic bowls. She took every chance to sample each and every aspect of life. Sometimes, she has tiptoed over the edge a little too far. However, she has always been able to bring herself back from the edge just in time. Often, I have been uncomfortable with how close Tarena always seems to teeter on the edge of danger and its unknown consequences. However, I have learned to trust that she has discovered her limits and will continue to develop her potential.

Chapter 16

Flames on the Mountain

The summer of 2002 offered a respite while I prepared to return for fall semester classes in health education after a 20-year nursing career. However, while reading an article in a Nevada nursing publication, I spotted an advertisement for a summer position as a camp nurse in the Colorado Rockies.

The magazine advertised a summer in the Rockies enjoying 600 acres of the lush, green, wooded mountains while caring for children between 7 and 17 years. These campers would spend the summer hiking, backpacking, and enjoying experiences that would help them acquire effective skills to become productive adults. I accepted the job as a camp nurse but didn't realize how much of an adventure I also would experience.

The two-day drive to the camp offered a restful, scenic sojourn. Although we could have driven to the camp site together, my husband decided at the last minute that he would drive his own car and follow me to the camp. It was a private, family-owned. It was a private, family-owned camp operating for the past 32 years outside the city limits of Durango, CO. The camp programs were well designed and outlined. All looked well, despite experiencing an unexpected bout of altitude sickness.

The historical culture of this camp required that the camp nurse be referred to as a "witch doctor" and the clinic as the "infirmary." So upon arrival to the camp and initial orientation, the witch doctor put the infirmary in order by scrubbing floors, placing sheets and wool blankets on metal-framed cots, washing windows, cleaning cobwebs, and inventorying medical supplies. I also needed to stock the 32 first-aid kits that the campers would be using on their wilderness back packing trips.

Bill didn't have an identified position at the camp. However, he had brought his video recorder along to camp and decided that he would tape the campers activities and they progressed. The camping staff was surprised to see him but after some negotiations everyone decided that a video history of the campers would be helpful. Bill was delighted that he would be able to navigate throughout the camp as needed to tape activities. He would have a very flexible schedule.

The third day brought organization to the camp programs. However, we had one last activity to complete—conducting a fire drill and reviewing the evacuation plan. These were finished without incident and in record time. Little did we know that we would be required to use our newly learned evacuation skills.

It was 9:30 p.m., and after an exhausting third day the camp was quiet. The urgent knock at my cabin door was greeted with surprise. Seeing one of the camp coordinators at our cabin elicited concern and anxiety. He was urging us to pack only my essential belongings and evacuate the camp. The intense flames of the Missionary Ridge forest fire had forced the local fire marshal to put the camp under a voluntary evacuation order. I looked out of the cabin window, and the ridge silhouette glowed orange with the intense fire. Only through cooperation and organization did we accomplish the monumental feat of contacting each camping group.

The vastness of the camp made contacting and organizing the campers a herculean task. Counselors and support staff maintained calm in a scary and potentially dangerous situation. All campers were notified and they filtered down the alluvial fans of the mountains to a pre-arranged central location. Once assembled, everyone assisted with packing and gathering needed supplies. Trying to locate Bill at this point was futile, I needed help with loading the jeep and organizing supplies – he was nowhere to be found.

At this point, we loaded into vans and were driven a few miles down the road to an open field. The coordinator of another area camp had offered their horse fields as a safe respite for the evacuees. Tents and tarps were erected, potable water was secured, restroom facilities were constructed with a leave-no-trace philosophy, nutritious snacks were provided by the Red Cross, and medical supplies were transported.

Camper medications were placed in locked fishing tackle boxes to be dispensed out of the back of a jeep by the "witch doctor." Medical supplies included a backboard, 32 first aid kits, individual medications, waterless hand sanitizer, duct tape, sports drinks, and a varied array of cotton balls, bandages, and assorted ointments and creams. An eclectic array of over-the-counter medications was assembled to address any emergency. I finally located Bill. He had made sleeping accomodations among a group of young, male camp counselors. He looked at me with clear defiance and stated that he intended to "stay with his buddies."

Even though we were momentarily safe, our initial retreat to the horse pasture was not the last refuge. The light of dawn revealed that most of the children had placed their bedrolls directly over piles of horse dung. This offered an additional challenge since there was no access to clean, running water to wash the sleeping attire. Some of the camp counselors came up with a unique solution. They hung the stinky, stained bedrolls over the fence to dry. When the manure encrusted bedrolls were dried, the camp counselors took large sticks from the surrounding unblemished trees and scrapped off the dried excrement.

Also, most of the younger children were still dressed in their sleeping attire, which they had been wearing for two days. You can imagine the site: a large group of various-aged, homesick children wandering through a dung littered horse pasture, dressed in their Mickey Mouse pajamas and teddy bear slippers, brushing off their manure encrusted sleeping bags.

On the third morning after the evacuation, the sky became smoke-filled and threatening. Smoke and ash from a steadily growing forest fire was enveloping the camp. Floating pieces of cinder burnt small holes in the tarp coverings and campers clothing. Staff members began experiencing symptoms of smoke inhalation: wheezing, shortness of breath, disorientation, burning eyes, and headaches. Four staff members were taken to the local emergency department. As we had done before, we packed our physical belongings and support supplies and organized our caravan for another road trip.

A local middle school, the second evacuation site, offered welcome relief. The air was clean, showers were available and campers could enjoy hot meals cooked in the school cafeteria. We slept on the hard gym floor, but at least, we were safe.

At this point, the camp coordinator decided to cancel the remainder of the camping season. We contacted the parents and began preparations to send the campers home. Small discussions groups convened to help the campers with their transition from camp to evacuation sites and then to home.

However, before the majority of the campers were scheduled to return home more changes were in store for the motley crew. Day two at the middle school brought new challenges for the camp coordinator in that he was notified that we would be moving again. The local Red Cross had designated the school site as an evacuation point for the local citizens. A few hundred fire evacuees were expected that afternoon. We were moving again to another school, our third evacuation site in as many days. Previous to all campers being sent home, Bill decided that he would leave the camp. He decided not to help with the closing.

Obviously, this was not the expected summer camp experience. Learning to be spontaneous in the wilderness was certainly a growing skill for me. I anticipated a defined routine during my camping life. What I received was a lesson in spontaneous adjustment and improvisation. I relearned lessons I thought that I already knew from the young children, who easily adjusted to uncertain situations. They were able to easily change their thoughts and actions in order to function well within constantly shifting situations. These children were beacons of change with little effort. They were examples of going with the flow. It was obviously stressful for them but they trusted the adults in charge and followed directions.

Leaving camp, I reflect on the memories of the summer. The vision of all the children wearing their Mickey Mouse bedroom slippers in the open field on the second day of fire evacuation will always be a cherished memory. Organizing the camper's medication out of the back door of a jeep was certainly challenging. However, the greatest lesson is the unintentional one the children taught me - that being open to change is a good thing. You're never too old to learn something new and fun at summer camp.

This however, was not the lesson that I learned from Bill. Obviously, he had used this camping experience to begin his physical separation from our marriage. I was surprised and confused about his behavior. Had he used this opportunity of spending the summer at camp to determine how he would feel about deserting his family? Reflecting on his separation need during our camping experience helps me to understand that Bill needed to separate from our family in stages and in deceitful ways. He was burning our relationship and evacuating our family structure much like our vacating the Missionary Ridge fire.

Chapter 17

Home Becomes Real Estate ... Again

Sometimes we meet people by chance because they are able to offer us a service when needed. That is how I met a special life-traveling companion who would walk with me through an extremely difficult time in life. My husband had recently died, and I was venturing into buying a home as a single woman. The real estate agent who walked with me on this journey was a companion, friend, soul mate, and a sister of the heart. She was a person who always answered my telephone calls no matter what the time of day. She walked with me down the dark, treacherous, foreboding, and stressful gauntlet of purchasing real estate as a single woman. Together, we found a house and transformed it into a home.

Picking just the right paint color for the living room wall had been the hardest decision. When it was finished, the memories of past tenants were hidden. Deciding on where to put my favorite picture was easier. The new vase I found fit well with my old, scratched, flowerpot. The house finally felt new, cozy, and welcoming, ready for me to call it home. Investing time and energy made each detail just right.

I hoped for a new start after my husband's death. It was a scary yet exciting process. Trepidation was my constant shadow as I walked through each detail of home ownership. As I positioned each item in just the right place, my thoughts drifted back to memories of the first house Bill and I had purchased together over thirty-five years ago. Remembering the birth of each of our three children, and the loss of our two other precious babies, focused me on the family events we had shared over the intervening years.

This nostalgia motivated my search through Bill's remaining possessions. I felt this final act could provide some closure, as well as a framework for a new start. A few weeks after his funeral, I finally had a quiet afternoon. This offered an opportunity to search through his personal effects. This could be the scene of emotional devastation or the opportunity to grasp onto elusive answers to nagging questions.

I remembered that Bill had been so angry in the last weeks before his death. He had cussed and yelled at me at each turn. He was not the man he had once been. What had made him so very angry? Was he hiding something? I hoped by reviewing these papers, it would provide insight into aspects of our life together that needed to be explored.

Searching through a briefcase filled with his business documents, I notice a piece of colored parchment paper carefully tucked into a side pocket. Under closer review, I realized that it was a handwritten note. As my fingertips traced the delicate edges of the folded note, I hesitated. I experienced a flashing feeling that reading the note would change my life, forever. The paper felt strangely sensual. It was obviously different from the business documents. Its soft texture has a welcoming, inviting touch. I hesitantly removed the document and unfold the expensive, scented paper. As I read, I realized that it was a tender, love note hand written by "him."

After thirty-five years of marriage, I knew Bill's handwriting intimately. I noted how he crossed his it's and used run-on sentences. My first thought was that the note was written for me and he didn't have time to give it to me before he had gotten so sick. But, as I read each tender word that he so purposely expressed and detected the bouquet whiffing up from the lightly scented parchment, I realized that the note was serenely composed for another woman, someone for whom he cared very deeply. He had a secret lover!

The words revealed a painful, devastating realization of betrayal. This truth seems to jump off of the page and slash at me with ravage reality. The words: *"I love you so very much sweetheart,"* explode off the page. The remnants fly up into my face as though they are radical pieces of shrapnel. My husband's betrayal occurred long ago, but I was just arriving at the intersection of truth and knowledge. This point in time was when I first became aware that I had been deceived. The revelation cut deeply because

Bill was the only person in my life that knew how to puncture my heart and burn my memories with sadness and grief forever.

Pulses of anger and devastation raged over my body. It was as if a huge wave punched through my body and threw me into a pulsating, uncontrollable whirlwind of hot, molten lava. I couldn't move, yet I was swirling. I couldn't understand. I still don't. The small, enclosed room began to spin and whirl as if there were an uncontrollable force in the room with me that had a preprogrammed direction and velocity.

Slowly, the hoodlum whirlwind began to give way to reason. The awareness of my body began to emerge from the erratic escapade. I began to feel the warm room temperature against my skin encasing my body. I slowly realized that there was the faint distracting noise of a car driving down the street coming from outside the window. I emerged back to the reverence of reality.

The only thought my brain activity could focus on was, why? Why had he been so reluctant to talk about it before he passed away? Did he feel guilty? How long had the affair been going on? Had the hint of suspicion been there, and had I ignored it?

Our parental structure, that fostered and cradled our precious children, had been a lie. Our life together was based on deceit. I pondered many questions. Sadly, there would never be any answers. The answers were buried with my husband under years of deceit, lies, and betrayals. How could any part of our life together be considered precious and true? I froze in time–encased in an iceberg. Unable to breathe or think, I was locked in the amber of our past.

I numbly walked to the bathroom. I splashed icy cold water on my face to shock my system, to dissipate this fantasy, this farce of discovery and wash it away. However, it didn't work. I stood there as if I were in the middle of a hurricane. The silence only offered a preview of the oncoming onslaught of biting, slashing, ravishing rain supported by equally destructive cutting and ripping winds. There was a permanent shift in the color of my world on that day.

I failed in my resolution to not cry. These tears did not flow from physical loss but betrayal of the heart. This cleansing Mecca of salty rain escaped from my broken heart, flooding my visual field. It was a testament that my clouded vision had been lifted. I tried to fight it. I was mad because

I didn't want to weep. My betrayer was not worth the effort. It would give credence that I had been yet wounded, again. My destitute dowager's heart crumbled. My portals of betrayal wept until my swollen, red puffy face no longer resembled my former reflection in the mirror.

My once strong and determined body with shoulders of an early pilgrim explorer's stature crumpled into a sunken framework of disarticulated bones holding reluctant flesh. My gaunt reflection in the bathroom mirror betrayed my mental memory. My former, trusting, naïve self was obliterated. It lay on the floor like shards of glass from a broken mirror, which no longer offered the happy, trusting reflection I so desperately craved.

I deflated onto the bathroom floor. My osteoporotic skeleton offered no resistance. My assaulted muscles contracted my hands and feet into a protective posture and curved my body inward to a fetal position. I sobbed uncontrollably. Devastated by a cathartic, painful realization, I lay exhausted on the bathroom floor swallowed in silence: my senses mute and unaware of time passage or activity. I had no realization of the changing light pattern filtering through the tiny bathroom window. My senses were numb to any and all outside stimulus. My body lay on the cold, hard unsympathetic bathroom floor, unresponsive.

The inner core of my being, the intangible thing that makes each of us a unique being, had been betrayed down to my inner core by someone that I had trusted with my life, my soul, and my secrets. Regrettably, now all the safety, security, and sense of accomplishment I had fought so very hard to restore in my life had evaporated. The opportunity for a fresh, new start was ruined. Not just a small betrayal had occurred but an insult deep into my very spiritual core - the "who" of me and "why" of me is threatened. Had our shared lives together been a lie? I could no longer rely on the glass-encased mercury of my trust thermometer. It had been crushed. The forsaken released metallic droplets were gliding without direction to unnamed destinations. I realized that things would not feel good again for a very, very, very long time.

I'm not sure just when my swollen eyes became aware of, and started to trace, the stark parallel patterns in the floor tiles. Ever so slowly I realized that I was lying on the bathroom floor and the room was dark and silent. My brain slowly started to relay a message to my exhausted body: *"I should get up. I* am *uncomfortable here."* That feeling of being uncomfortable would follow me, possess me, and consume me for a very long time to come.

Then, as always, days and time tick-tock slowly and painfully by and by and by. The world does not wait for anyone who has experienced a devastating blow. It does not care. It marches through grief and despair as though it were enjoying a sunny, breezy afternoon in the park. If I was going to gather the strength and fortitude to drag my partially comatose body off of that bathroom floor, I was going to have to do it alone. The task was accomplished in a blur of exhaustion and half-hearted determination.

Each succeeding day, I mustered my courage and mentally enticed myself into the delusion that life was worth living. Slowly, and oh so very painfully, I began talking to my inner self. *"I must move on. I must drag myself out of this defeated and humbled mode."* Although my spirit was very reluctant, time moved on without my input as if I was disconnected from reality. Numbness to daily activities threatened to construct a large, pit-encrusted wall between me and everyone I loved. It was like being in a tunnel. I could see busy people carrying out their chores at the far end, but I was rigidly encased in solitude at the other end– never interacting or being part of the activity. My inner recovering spirit encouraged me to muster strength. Even though it is stingy and fragile, a small inner voice keeps whispering to me *"I need to keep busy, keep my body moving."* I must work through the fact that I had been betrayed down to the smallest fiber of my inner self.

Working through a betrayal requires either immersion into an intentional and calculated program of recovery or an unaware drifting through humanity as though one were injected with Novocain. I chose a thoughtful recovery program. I decided to start exercising at the gym again. Physical movement helped me to resolve past challenges, and it offered some solace now. Some days I would finish my workout at the gym and be completely exhausted - other days I would barely start an easy exercise routine and be overcome with exhaustion.

Exercise seemed to offer an opportunity to refresh my body and permitted my mind to go into automatic pilot. Somehow I just had to keep going. I had to allow my body and spirit to heal. Life experience had taught me that keeping busy with everyday life and staying physically active were the keys for me. I needed time to sort out the signals my body was sending me. *"Taking cues from my body"* was the answer. I had already learned this lesson.

One day after completing an especially good workout my body felt vaguely different. My body didn't respond as expected. Identifying the elusive feeling was difficult. My muscles and joints were in conflict. Awakening the next morning, I noted that my hands and feet were swollen and my joints ached. My toes felt tight and looked like large sized cotton balls. Something wasn't right: I just didn't feel well. Rationalizing that I had been through some very stressful situations in the past few months, I decided rest would be my only escape.

Weeks passed the symptoms remained. Being a registered nurse for thirty years, I tended to "self-diagnose." However, this was a different matter. Ignoring my suspicions could kill me. This situation needed a medical intervention. My life was about to take yet another devastating turn and this time I would not so easily recover.

Numerous medical tests and multiple doctor reports confirmed my worst suspicions. I was diagnosed with systemic lupus, rheumatoid arthritis, Charcot Marie tooth disease, fibromyalgia, neuropathy, Reynaud's and a variety of other autoimmune medical conditions. Active symptoms of these conditions made each body movement painful and difficult. It was a cascading watershed of medical problems, stumbling down on me like buckets of bricks targeted at cracking my resolve and endurance.

My doctors explained that these autoimmune conditions were programmed into my DNA, the building block of my basic genetic being. Symptoms of these conditions are triggered by stressful events. I became an ambulatory appendage of medical conditions. Obviously, the stress of my husband's betrayal threatened to shackle me to a life of pain and anguish.

"Why me? Why now?" The old questions arose because I was just beginning to make progress. Life wasn't fair, and I had become accustomed to its unforgiving twists and turns. Still I wondered how the tide could turn in such a negative direction at this time in my life. I was a grandmother, my children were grown, and I should be able to enjoy this time of my life.

Life enjoyment was not to be. How could I work each day and bear the pain and stiffness radiating throughout every tense, pulsating fiber of my body? It was as if my husband's skeletal hand reached up from the grave and pulled me down into the cold, black, unforgiving, devouring shroud of dirt. He tethered me to his betrayal by an invisible iron ball and chain. My cheating, deceitful husband had welded me to his memory with the hot, molten fire of debilitating disease and chronic fatigue. Even in death he showed his betraying hand of cards. He made sure that we were bonded "till death do us part."

Monthly chemotherapy infusions were used to decrease the activity of my crippled immune system. My morning medication routine included a variety of pills aimed at reducing my symptoms: radiating pain, intense fatigue, and general muscle wasting. Nothing would cure the multitude of chronic, debilitating diseases assaulting my body. Not only would I have to deal with the multiple symptoms but the debilitating side effects of multiple medications as well. It was obvious; I would have to medically retire. I would lose my income along with my ability to secure an income. I would lose my newly purchased home.

The precious home that was a beacon of a new start would disappear from my life. I had just finished placing all of my precious items in just the right place. I had finally achieved a comfortable and safe feeling, and then my universe crumbled before me! My hard fought resolve grew fragile and cracked. Then, it was simply swept away.

I begrudgingly removed the pictures from the wall. I wrapped up my favorite vase. I gave the flowerpot to my new neighbor who had always loved it. I packed up my clothes, dishes, and computer. I threw away all the odds and ends that would now be of little use–personal items that make a house into a home. I also got rid of all the items that reminded me of my unfaithful life partner. I called the real estate agent who had worked so diligently with me and let her know that the house was again available for sale. The home would become real estate, once again.

Months later, during the sale of the house, my friend and realtor died of a chronic disease. She had also been trying to manage a fatal medical condition and yet she had shielded her clients from her own aggressive struggle. However, her battle was now complete.

I tried to make sense of all the challenges that I had faced in the past years. Sometimes you just need a companion to walk with you down the treacherous road of betrayal and deceit–someone who will listen to you and offer the precious gift of friendship. My real estate agent, Linda, was there just at the right time to offer comfort and advice. I wish that I had known about her medical challenge so that I would have been available to somehow help her along her path.

The sale of my house was transferred to another realtor who proved to be every bit as competent and concerned as L. J., the new realtor, completed the paperwork in a professional manner, and we became friends in the process. The real estate was sold to a young family who was searching to make a house into a home.

Chapter 18

Thieves

When you turn off the lights at home at night and all is quiet, the scene is set for the heist. Dark-clad thieves silently, under the shadow of distortion, enter your vulnerable home and confiscate your most precious items– articles which help define your lifestyle and family memories. The pieces of daily life, to which you attach an internal emotional conversation, are stolen. This crime is punishable by the legal system. Hopefully, they will be judged by the evidence and held accountable. Repentant thieves will serve their debt to society and reenter the populous as healthy contributing citizens.

My personal thieves snuck into my life when my emotional lights were extinguished.

When I noticed some small, tinted, perfumed sheets wedged in the side pocket of his briefcase, the emotional, amorous pledge divulged on those last bits of paper devastated my life. As I read the searing words they crushingly revealed an affectionate, yet veiled, love affair between my husband and a woman he met through his job in Ohio. My knowledge of this illicit devotion attacked not only my brain and heart with its intensity but my defense system and immune resistance as well. Thus, the thieves of illness were allowed to enter my emotionally darkened body.

The searing realization of the love-lorn words cloaked my immune system in dark shadows of distortion, much like the late night uninvited intruders in a darkened room. These invaders, these marauders, surrounded, attacked, and weakened my defenseless health perimeter. My psyche knew that my heart had been assaulted and the damage was uncompensable. It took many diagnostic tests and multiple office visits to connect the names of the marauders to their identifying personalities.

My nursing background gave me a medical understanding of the destructive process that was occurring within my body. Emotional trauma stresses the body and triggers a myriad of cascading events. O'Shea et al. identified an immune system gene called BACH2: "This gene is a critical regulator of the immune system's reactivity." [10] This system's reactivity struggles for cell repair. When "self-healing" occurs, the body returns to homeostasis–a state of well being. This hidden inner-war is called the antigen-antibody loop. The antigen–an outside substance–stimulates an immune response. It is like creating an invisible shield for the immune system so that if the substance invades the body at some later date it is recognized and a defense is mounted. Therefore, the person will not become sick by the substance.

However, if the damage is too intense and if the repair efforts are insufficient, the patient dies. In my case, the patient, my immune system, was attacked by an antiballistic missile and died. A hallmark of this annihilation is inflammation. This excessive combustion caused tissue, nerve, and muscle damage. The emotional attack, brought on by my husband's unfaithfulness and emotional betrayal, was so complete that my inflamed immune system never recovered. In fact, a major flaw in my immune system was revealed by this major stressor. That is, in my DNA (deoxyribonucleic acid) structure there was the potential for developing a multitude of autoimmune diseases. This characteristic was expressed when my system was exposed to intense and multi-faceted pressure. The disease process provided the framework for the identifying personalities of the thieves.

---

[10] Roychoudhuri, R., Hirahara, K., Mousavi, K., Clever, D., Klebanoff, C. A., Bonelli, M., Sciume, G., Zare, H., Vahedi, G., Dema, B., Yu, Z., Liu, H., Takahashi, H., Rao, M., Muranski, P., Crompton, J. G., Ounkosdy, G., Bedongnetti, D., Wang, E., Hoffman, V., Rivera, J., Marincola, F. M., Nakamura, A., Sartorelli, V., Kanno, Y., Gattinoni, L., Muto, A., Igarashi, K., O'Shea, J. J., and Restifo, N.P. (2013) BACH2 represses effector programs to stabilize T(reg)-mediated immune homeostasis. Nature, 498(7455), 506-510. doi: 10.1038/nature12199

Every band of thieves has an authority at the helm—a mastermind who designs the success of the attack. The leader of the pack determines the structure of the robbery. He designs the plan that provides entry for the invaders. The leader of the marauders assures the success of the robbery. This leader, this mastermind, this designer of destruction was none other than my Bill. He was my "Mr. Wonderful." He provided the design for the thieving knaves. Bill's betrayal so depleted my ability to defend myself both physically and emotionally that the physiological door, the living matter within myself, was left wide open and unlocked. The band of thieves simply walked in the front door.

These thieves, like any other shady characters, had adopted nicknames in order to disguise their true identities. They would be known as a family but each would adopt a different strand of DNA within the family bloodline. The family name was baptized "Autoimmune." The head of the family was christened by me "Son Of A Bitch" (previously known as Mr. Wonderful) with individual members receiving irreverent Christian designations such as Systemic Lupus Erythematosus, Rheumatoid Arthritis, Charcot Marie Tooth Disease, Raynaud Syndrome, Connective Tissue Disease, Fibromyalgia, Antiphospholipid Antibodies and a myriad of other debilitating names. These medical designations produce proteins from specialized B-cells after stimulation of an antigen in an immune response. This basically means that my immune system, which normally would protect me from invading viruses and bacteria, mutated. My immune system was now volatile. Unfortunately, my unsuspecting normal body systems were targeted by the invading entities. My hyper-vigilant immune system was working overtime, desperately trying to eliminate me.

Waking up one morning brought strange sensation in my hands and feet. I lay in the foggy state of waking slumber trying to discern the relevance of the feelings. Looking at my hands and feet, I realized that all of my appendages were swollen. Stiffness and joint tenderness signaled that it would be a challenging struggle to get out of bed and dress for work. Indeed, it took an extra hour to accomplish the task and resulted in me being late for work. I made an appointment with my primary care provider for an examination.

"You have a variety of autoimmune diseases, and we will continue to do more testing," the doctor said after reviewing my laboratory results and completing a physical examination.

I felt my head shake from side to side as if I were trying to ward off a pesky gnat interrupting a restful slumber. No matter how I shook my head, the words kept repeating in my ears. As a practicing registered nurse, I fully understood what the doctor was saying. I just couldn't accept that she was saying those words to me. I was a healthy, active, professional person. I couldn't be sick. I didn't have time. In an instant, my life changed! My heart knew that my life would be different from that day forward. My soul was scarred, forever.

I lost myself in every way that a person can be lost. Idealist memories of my thirty-five year marriage were gone. My healthy body was sick. My perception of "self" was murdered. The naïve trust in mankind had been mortally betrayed. My world smothered in black! It had all been accomplished in a stealth attack by betrayal of a loved one. My drive home from the doctor's office was filled with swirling thoughts and a foggy environment of disbelief and self-talk. I went down standing up!

The next few months were a whirlwind of doctor appointments and medical tests. My primary care doctor prescribed copious amounts of medication to decrease the pain, swelling, and inflammation. She referred me to a variety of medical specialist including a cardiologist, rheumatologist, endocrinologist, neurologist, and pulmonologist. Each could treat the medical complications that would be occurring within my body's internal organs, but no one could repair my broken heart. What I was observing on the outside of my body–swelling, inflammation, stiffness–was also assaulting the inside of my body. I didn't feel the same. I didn't sleep as soundly. My perception of sound changed. Eating was a challenge. My taste buds betrayed me, and nothing tasted normal. I couldn't walk or move without pain.

My previous life was topsy-turvy. Nothing fit into my life pattern as it had before. My body ached all over and nothing relieved the discomfort. My mind was blurry. My muscles ached, and I was exhausted. I couldn't believe it had all happened so quickly. I realized that my husband had left me with not only the psychological darkness of marital betrayal, but the everyday physical pain of chronic disease. I had been fucked in every way that a person can be –physically, emotionally, psychologically, and socially. I would carry the social scar of betrayal, forever.

I imagine the heist was so complete because the thieves were so accomplished. Their ringleader, "Mr. Wonderful," was a master at hiding his true motives. He had always shown, to me, the face of a family man–a father who loved his children. I felt that he loved me as his wife.

I had always heard that when a husband is cheating on his wife there are suggestive signs. Little signals that betray the husband's secret actions, such as: staying late at the office on a regular basis or a sudden increase in spending on jewelry that had never been apparent in the husband/wife relationship. I had not detected any of this behavior prior to my husband's betrayal. He had been very adept at hiding his deceitful actions since he was living in Ohio and he had sent his bank statements to his sister. Obviously, my husband had been quite adept at all of these activities. Until the moment that I found the love notes, I had trusted him (Bill) – totally. My trust was so complete that I had no second thoughts about him the pet name of "Mr. Wonderful."

The leader of the gang did his job very well. He gained my trust and broke down my defenses completely. My stressed immune system exploded. I was defenseless. I was vulnerable to disease and disability. The stage was set for my DNA potential to invade the scene.

They, the crew of thieves, the autoimmune diseases, observed as the ringleader dressed in his finery, took a long, deep and slow bow of acknowledgement for his accomplishment then they entered the open door to begin robbing my body of its precious reserves. They were very adept at their job and expressed their destructive force in measured doses.

Systemic lupus erythematosus attacked my muscles and inflicts different degrees of destruction. Similarly, rheumatoid arthritis assaulted my joint function and impeded my muscle strength with debilitating fatigue. Fibromyalgia struck without warning filling different sections of my body with intense pain that often rendered a limb useless. Antibodies, which formed blood clots in the circulatory system, hid in the DNA dark shadows anxiously threatening me. Charcot Marie Tooth Disease a progressive, neurological, debilitating disease decreases feeling and function of my hands and feet. Neuropathy convinces me that my hands and feet are shooting out hot burning flames from the tips.

Unfortunately, the thieves are astute students and studied well the habits of the ringleader. The stage, the marital betrayal, offered the opportunity for them to burst onto the scene and angrily release their venom into my system. Within a very short time, I was not only physically uncomfortable but restricted to a daily medication routine. Every joint, muscle, tendon, and circulatory system in my body was under attack. I screamed uncle, but No one heard and no one cared. My doctors, and there were many, keep prescribing medications, and the diagnostic centers keep testing.

The future looks the same – doctor visits, medication, diagnostic tests and blood draws. It is safe to say that when my cheating husband passed away, he took a large part of me with him. I learned that all men cheat because they can, either emotionally or physically. That is not to say that all men are scum or are dirty. It is just a fact that is true for me. It may not be so for another woman but it is my reality.

Naïve trusting is not part of my daily life. I now tentatively trust on a superficial basis until I can verify with facts. I have learned that once a person lies, they will always lie. I realize that each time I lumber through a challenging situation it robs more of the me that constitutes the person that I am. Each time I face a tough situation, I am less able to deal with the next tough situation—believe me there is always a next tough situation.

I learned by observing my children that their reality of their father was different than my reality of my husband. They jealously hold on to jaded childhood memories of a shrouded individual who intermittently offered cloaked remnants of affection. In their eyes, he was a good father. However, he was not a good man. He was not a good husband. It has been a difficult decision for me-should I tell my children about their father's marital betrayal? I know that I risk shattering their memories of their father. Will they find out about his girl friend on their own? Will another family member tell them? Will they find out years from now at a family function and realize that I have known "the secret" for many years and didn't share it with them? Will I hurt them more by not telling them what I know? These are all very difficult questions.

I agonize about whether or not to tell my children! Time relinquished its grip as the weeks passed. I decided to relate the incident of discovering the love notes in my husband's briefcase to my oldest daughter.

"Can I see the note?" She asked. The darting look in her eyes said, *"I don't believe you."*

I realized that I was threatening the image of her beloved father. I explained to her that in my rage of discovery, *"I shredded the note and flushed it down the toilet."*

She instantly averted my eye contact. Instinctively, I knew that my daughter would never truly trust me again. She would never confide her most trusted thoughts in me again. No matter what, even in death, she would always and forever believe and trust her beloved father. She convinced herself, in a fleeting instant, that I was lying. Even in death, my husband robbed me of my children's love and affection. No matter what I did or said after that microsecond of reality, my relationship with my daughter would never be as it once was.

When I told my youngest daughter about the note, she was emotionally devastated, but I at least I knew that she believed me. She trusted and loved her father to a fault. He was her knight in shining armor. Her father was the one who would rescue her from any and all dangers in this unforgiving world. I knew that it hurt her heart! A fragile piece of her died that day. She judged all men by the example that her father set, and her exemplar was now a shattered specimen of broken shards dissipated on the hard floor.

Telling my son about his father's love note was a task that I left for last - simply because I sensed that he would react with physical violence. When he gets mad, he can get physically violent.

Somehow, the sense of betrayal is greater when a son hears about his father's betrayal. I still struggle to put that father-son relationship into words. Maybe, it's because I'm not a man. Maybe, it just seems worse when the knife of truth slices so close to the bone.

I had little reserve to deal with the issue either physically or physiologically. When he heard my words he was silent for a few moments. It was as if he had been punched in the gut and couldn't believe that he didn't see it coming. He started yelling at me, calling me a liar and every nasty word and phrase that a pimp in a back street bar would utter. I waited silently until he was done. He was deeply hurt to the depth of his soul. I also detected, by a slight fleeting spark in his eye, that he might have known some small facts about his father's other life. He didn't share whatever he knew. I didn't even ask him about it because I couldn't endure the answer.

The final convincing act of their fathers' betrayal came a few weeks later. While searching through Bill's briefcase, I discovered a bank slip from an Ohio bank. It listed a deposit for $100.00, my husband's name, a bank ID number, and a 1-800 phone number for the bank. It was a small, unassuming piece of paper that could have easily been missed by a less-suspicious eye. Examining the receipt closely, I saw that the name of the bank and the ID number were not familiar.

I called the number. The receptionist on the phone was reluctant to provide information about the bank account since I couldn't provide her with the needed security screening information. However, I pursued the conversation and convinced the bank manager that I was the account holder's wife. I was able to learn that the bank account was in my husband's name, that he opened it when he began work in Ohio, and that my name was not on the account. I couldn't get any further information. The bank manager informed me that if I wanted additional information, I would have to provide a legal, certified document indicating that: I was the account holder's wife; I was married to him at the time of his death, and that he had died. I provided the documents.

The second call to the bank was shocking.

"Where are the monthly statements for the account being sent?" I asked, figuring that if I knew this information then I would know the name and address of my husband's girlfriend.

"The name and address on the bank statement is somewhere in Illinois." My surprise was complete. The statements were sent to my husband's sister in Small Town. I also learned that if I wanted access to the funds in the account, I needed to secure documents from the State of Nevada and Ohio verifying that I was processing my late husband's estate.

My appearance in Nevada civil court procured the documents. When the postman handed me the certified envelope from the Ohio bank, I signed the release form with a shaky hand. I tenaciously clenched the document. It was the one, true physical testament of betrayal.

In a fit of rage I had destroyed the hidden love note – the evidence of betrayal - but I wouldn't demolish this confirmation. Oddly, it was my only physical bastion. I carefully examined the envelope only half believing its validity. Turning the envelope over in my hands several times helped me to verify its' validity. Questioning my sense of sight, sound and touch was important since I had been so easily betrayed by my husband for the past thirty-five years of marriage.

I considered calling my children and informing them that the check arrived, but I hesitated. This was a moment of privacy and solitude. I suspected that it could be the first step in my healing process. I opened the envelope–the veil of my bastion. It was a check. It bore my name. I sat and sobbed.

My hearts conscious whispered to me to give it away. I struggled to ignore the solicitation. The funds could help pay off the intense, tardy debt that remained from my husband's shiftlessness. However, I also knew that having the money from the bank account would help substantiate the entire horrible, ridiculous, repulsive situation for my children. I wanted them to know the truth. More importantly, I ached for them to believe the truth. I offered the money to my children. They accepted with regret and consummation.

This situation delayed the mourning process for me. The energy I needed to understand my husband's marital betrayal consumed all of my resources. The artifacts of that battle had scarred every system of my being. The ringleader, my husband, and band of thieves, my resulting chronic diseases, robbed me of my ability to complete the mourning process. What is more important, I acknowledged that I carried the grief. This issue peppered my daily activities and influenced my choices. My children still find it difficult to discuss their father, but it is obvious that they are still grieving for their image of the perfect dad.

Needless to say, when I am in the dark these days I always set my alarm and have a weapon at my side. I can detect and deter any thieves who may want to steal my few precious possessions. The accused thieves in this saga have been tried. The verdict was that they were found wanting and guilty. Sadly, they will never pay for their offenses. They will never be held accountable or be required to repent for their transgressions. They have gotten off "scott-free." The nebulous thieves came under the cover of darkness, completed the premeditated heist and escaped with the plundered possessions. The innocent victims –me and my precious children–have paid dearly for the atrocious crimes. I know that our lives are forever changed, and my children have lost the pride and adoration they once had for their father.

Chapter 19

Hello, Affection, Desire

This poem was a gift to my current husband. It relates our relationship from the first meeting as a potential couple to eventual marriage. I presented it to him on our first wedding anniversary. Finding love the second time around can be both wonderful and unexpected. There were my feelings as I began my life together with my second husband, Spencer. Our relationship began simply by chance, or destiny, I'm not sure.

HELLO, AFFECTION, DESIRE

Meeting and greeting is how it began,
For a girl named Joyce
And a boy named Van.

Waiting and searching each one's soul
Tentatively wondering if they should risk the adventure
And seek out the goal.
Life experiences had taught them to wait -
Like checking out the water before you jump in the lake.
If only this time, the feeling would grow. Maybe the heart would truly know.

They learned together what things seemed to flow.
Tried new experiences and learned as their commitment would grow.

The seasons and time passed almost seamlessly,
As the two individuals seemed to become–we.

She likes faster and shopping and finding new things,
He is content and watchful like waiting to see if the beautiful bird sings.
Caution is wise when mixed with adventure,
The two seemed destined but who could conjecture.

Each experience and encounter offered more space
For feelings and thoughts to take their own place.
Affection and caring, closeness and sharing,
Like fruit of a tree in spring that starts bearing.

It appears certain, as time passes on, that the we
Has developed -
From the original you and me.

Love has developed, trust has established, and friendship is true,
I offer this poem simply to say, "I LOVE YOU."

****

My oldest daughter, during a Sunday afternoon visit, suggested that I investigate some of the computerized dating options that exist for older adults. She had noticed that settling into widowhood had been an adjustment for me. Initially, I dismissed the idea as a foolishness best left for the younger women who had the time and inclination to display their lives and interests to the public eye for review. I had an established career and grown children to occupy my time. However, she was persistent and continued to arouse my curiosity with tidbits of information about her girlfriends' adventures that had begun through computerized dating services.

On a rainy Sunday afternoon, I decided to just peek at this new rage of online dating. I logged-on to the recommended computer site, and it piqued my interest to the point that time passed unnoticed. I spent an hour scrolling through online profiles of individuals but it only felt like minutes. Obviously, I was hooked. I wasn't going to sit on a bar stool and entice drunks in order to meet potential future partners, nor was I going to go to the local grocery store and squeeze the produce in order to meet Mr. Right. However, I was interested in creating a personal profile filled with my likes and interests in order to meet someone who would enjoy going to an afternoon movie or spending an evening sharing a nice dinner.

When I began checking for matches, there seemed to be a multitude of prospects from which to choose, and I started dating. It was another learning experience. Of course, I observed all of the safety precautions–meeting in safe places, withholding personal information, being aware of my surroundings.

Conversations with the men I met were stimulating and activities were enjoyable. Unfortunately, each new man that I met seemed to be preoccupied with quickly finding a pretty young thing and flying off to a tropical island for enjoyment. Personal connections and honest friendship were not on their agenda. Disillusionment stalked me as the months passed. Finally, on a Sunday night just as I was headed to bed, I decided to check the site one last time. The picture of a new profile appeared on my computer screen, and I was immediately drawn to his popping blue eyes. They seemed to twinkle. He wasn't dashing or exceedingly rich, but he certainly had a quality that attracted me enough to investigate his dating profile. We met and I discovered a kind, truthful, intelligent and loving man who had himself been widowed a few years past. In fact, we discovered that even though we lived in the same neighborhood we had never met. We met each other at a local shopping mall during a busy Saturday morning because all of the dating specialists advise you to pick an open area where there are lots of people to meet. If Spencer could last for a few hours of trekking through the feminine-based apparel and sweet-smelling novelty shops, I should be able to venture into comic book stores and man-cave specialty locations. By the end of the day, a tall, good looking, middle-aged man emerged from the mall proudly carrying a variety of femininely decorated, sweet-smelling, multi-colored bags. His evident smile announced his even temperament and his joyful mood. Obviously, he had an enjoyable afternoon. His accompanying lady – me, carried a wee bag containing a baseball hat with a Green Bay Packers logo. We both walked toward our adjacent cars, hand-in-hand.

We dated for two years. During this time, my children seemed to be unsure about what position Spencer Van Walters would hold in our family structure. I'm sure that this was confusing for them. When it became obvious that our relationship was developing into a lifelong, sharing partnership, Spencer proposed marriage. I initially hadn't entertained the idea of entering into another relationship. I wondered if I could trust other people in general and men in specific.

I also had to be honest with Van and tell him that I had been diagnosed with a plethora of debilitating autoimmune medical conditions. This would affect our everyday lives together. Van and I talked extensively about our past, and I discovered that his departed wife had also been diagnosed with the exact same debilitating medical conditions and that the complications of those conditions had indeed caused her death. This meant that he was aware of the health challenges I would encounter as my condition progressed. It meant that I could well die in the same manner as his first wife. He personally knew the horrible ravages of the debilitating autoimmune diseases. The process could be quick or painfully slow. He had accompanied his wife through the terminal process. The future was definitely uncertain.

Van and I discussed these issues at length. I explained about the new interventions that had proven to be highly effective while admitting the setbacks I already experienced. I had learned from my first marriage that truth is always the best and first adage. He was surprisingly open and available to an in-depth discussion about personal issues. It was refreshing and a little scary for me. My previous partner had not been willing to openly discuss his feelings and issues. This unwillingness had plunged our relationship into secrets and betrayal. Spencer and I would have to base our partnership on love and respect for each other if our union was going to lead to marriage.

Accompanied by our children, Van and I were married in June of 2009 on the top of Mount Charleston in Las Vegas, Nevada. Since that time, we have been a happy couple and a united family.

Chapter 20

The Teachable Moment...

My ten-year old granddaughter and I were spending one of those wonderful, interactive afternoons talking about the type of telephone I used when I was a child. She had just gotten her new cellular phone, and I thought it would be a good opportunity to talk to her about my old fashioned telephone.

I proceeded to explain how it was a rotary telephone with a two-pronged device attached to the wall by an electrical cord. One portion of the telephone was a number-oriented, rotary-dial pad attached to a heavy, plastic base. The other component was a speaker/receiver assembly attached with an extension wire to the main, number-oriented rotary dial pad. The dial pad had a circular rotating wheel with smaller inner circles placed clockwise on it. Each inner circle corresponded to a given number—such as 1-2-3-4 etc.

I explained that if you wanted to make a call, you would confirm the number of the person that you wanted to call and then locate the corresponding numbers on the inner circular dial. You would then place finger into the circular hole and rotate the dial around in a clock-wise direction to a stop. When you removed your finger from the circle, the circular wheel would return to its original position automatically.

For example, you would put your finger into circle number three, spun the inner circle around to the stop for number three, and then let the dial return to its original position. After this, you would select your next number in the series and perform the function again until all the numbers within the telephone number had been dialed. Because the device was stationary, you could not carry it around with you as you talked. There usually was a designated place on the kitchen counter or wall for the phone. Sometimes a special piece of furniture called a telephone stand would be placed in the hallway or living room where the telephone could be set for easy access.

Each area of the United States had specific numbers and letters assigned to it so that the person making a call to Chicago, Illinois would have a number such as CHI 2-3-4-5. Initially, all telephone numbers contained both numbers and letters. A centralized station telephone operator would assist you to make the call by dialing the numbers and letters for you. This however, would allow that centralized person to listen in on your private conversations. Customers also had the option of being on a party line where they shared their phone line time with a number of other telephone users in their neighborhood.

This meant that if someone was using the telephone when you wanted to make a call, you would have to wait until their call was completed to initiate yours. This could be a few minutes or sometimes much longer. The home telephone was often considered a luxury that some home owners couldn't afford. In this case, the person would use a centrally located neighborhood telephone that might be located in the closest grocery store or at the most convenient gas station. The employees at these community locations would take the phone call for designated neighbors and then relay the message as soon as possible. Sometimes they would even send a store employee to the person's home to relay the phone message.

The home telephone was also considered a nuisance by many. Therefore, some people would use the phone only in the case of an emergency. If you got a phone call, it was considered a very important event. It usually was to relay special information such as the medical condition of a family member or upcoming special events such as a birthday or wedding.

After I had spent what I thought was a good amount of time explaining to my granddaughter my experiences with the telephone, I expected some expression of wonder or excitement from her. Instead, as I looked at my granddaughter who was now squirming in her chair and said *"So, what do you think?"*

"Grandma, why didn't you just use your cell phone?" She asked impatiently, turning her head slightly to the side and squinting eyes.

About two weeks after this encounter, I received a telephone call from my daughter.

"Guess what mom?" she asked. *"We found an old rotary telephone that you were talking about the other day. I showed your granddaughter what it looked like. She wasn't impressed."*

"Where did you find a rotary phone?" I asked.

"It was in this cute, little, old antique shop." After this conversation with my granddaughter, I will never look at a telephone quite the same way again…

This interaction forcefully reminded me that each person perceives a situation through their own eyes and the influences of their past experiences. Since my granddaughter had never seen, or even used, a rotary telephone there was no possible way she, at her tender age, could have understood my experience of making phone calling with a rotary phone in the "good ole' days."

Her frame of reference was modern day, electric and digital. There was no space in her brain for the thought of slow, methodical and old. This experience also refreshed for me the understanding that as I "listen" to people who interact with me in my life that particular person may well not know, or worse even care, what the effects their actions may have on me. In reality, most people could care less – they focus on themselves.

However, I can't stress enough that every day and in every way each persons' actions are and do influence others. Someone is always listening. The line of listening is always being written.

Chapter 21

I Kudd'a Be'n Sum'body

Rod Steiger (The Gent) and Marlon Brando (Terry Malloy) in the 1954 crime movie "On the Waterfront" were sitting in the cushioned back seat of a car discussing activities of the Manhattan and Brooklyn longshoremen's union. These two brothers were opposing bastions of union activities. Steiger was the enforcer of the undercover details and dealings that occurred in order for the workers to receive special treatment for job assignments. Brando was involved in the opposite venue: the day-to-day inter-workings of the longshoremen. He had a raw and realistic understanding of daily life among dock workers: He lives it. However, Brando was disillusioned and angry. He had compromised his promising boxing career at the request of his brother. Brando saw his own activities slowly mirroring his brother's enforcement activities, and he hated himself for it. Both brothers were trapped by their decisions.

Tension in the cushioned car was claustrophobic. Brando turned toward his older brother and painfully, half pleadingly states, *"I kudda be'n sumbody."* He realized that his chance of capturing and holding on to his pride as a man, as a person, and as a successful, professional boxer was forever gone. Not only that, but the promise was gone—the promise from his brother for protection. At the bequest of Steiger, Brando surrendered his promising career with a fixed fight so that his older brother's boss could profit. Brando cried his plea again with despair, *"I kudd'a be'n sum'body. I kudd'a be'n sum'body."*

This is my mindset, my feeling, as I sat in the infusion chair in the endocrinologist office. I was receiving another dose of a biologic chemotherapy that destroys the activity of my mutated immune system. This drug counteracted the activity of rheumatoid arthritis and systemic lupus erythematosus. I experienced a watershed of medical changes within my body since receiving the diagnosis. My nursing background was helpful for researching the symptoms of these autoimmune diseases. Psychological stress in my life depleted my coping ability. That, in turn, negatively affected my body functions. My immune system exploded, expressing my DNA potential to develop these extreme medical diseases. The chronic stress on my body was taking its' toll.

Juxtaposed to the process of dealing with my husband's betrayal, I was notified that my mother was within days of death. She suffered from chronic diseases and a lingering illness, but the actuality of her death caught me emotionally unprepared. I was in the throes of emotional distress: mourning for both the loss of my husband and his marital intimacy. There seemed little capacity to accommodate another intense loss. However, phone conversations with my sister concerning our mother's illness related that death was imminent.

My trip to Illinois gave me time to mentally recognize my mother's life. She died September 12, 2005. Following the funeral, per my mother's request, we transported her ashes to Nebraska for internment next to her parents. In order to accommodate the trip, I needed to secure additional days of leave from my nursing employment. I contacted H,[11] my nursing supervisor, informed her of the situation, and requested additional leave. She refused the request and told me that if I wanted to take extra time to make the trip to bury my mother, I would have to quit my job.

"I quit if that is my only option," I stated with determination. It became yet another extremely stressful situation. Eventually, my supervisor granted my additional leave request. However, upon returning to work, I was transferred to another workstation.

Entering a new work area was also a stressful situation. Working as a clinic based nurse for the Veteran's Administration hadn't prepared me for the military hospital setting on an air force base. Intense dedication to

---

[11]   Name changed.

duty certainly helped me to adjust. My new nursing supervisor was non-appreciative and demanding – depleting all my physical and emotional reserve. After a few months, I was feeling the effects of intense stress emanating from attempting to learn the unwritten rules that governed my new work environment. Fatigue overwhelmed me, my muscles ached and cramped without apparent reason and my entire body experienced shooting chills alternating with warm flushing waves throughout my body without notice or reason. Even with increased periods of rest, I experienced no relief from fatigue.

After a few months, activity in my life seemed to be downgraded to normal. I felt as though I could take some enjoyment in daily activities such as returning to my normal exercise routine and interacting with a few trusted friends. However, normal was not to be part of life from this point until eternity. Awakening one morning I noted that my hands and feet were tingling and swollen and I was tired to the point of exhaustion as though I had climbed a very tall mountain while asleep. My first thought was that I had been bitten by a bug and it had caused an allergic reaction. Then I thought I was having a systemic reaction to something I had eaten. Every movement I performed to get my body out of bed brought me intense pain. My body was struck still with panic!

Every part of my body hurt and was stiff. It had occurred overnight. My swollen body had morphed into a life-sized sausage. Struggling to find nursing shoes that were two sizes larger than normal so that I could fit my swollen, puffy feet into my shoes for work was a painful endeavor. My fingers resembled enlarged hot dogs. I felt that if I tried to clench my fist my fingertips would break open and the tender flesh inside would eviscerate. I was afraid that my body would keep swelling. I couldn't imagine what had gone wrong.

The year 2008 brought increased intensity to my new normal. This was when the doctors diagnosed my youngest daughter with kidney failure due to lupus complications. They offered her either kidney dialysis or a kidney transplant to keep her alive. The discussion and decision process for our family involved heated, intense, and emotional conversations.

To make matters worse, once she chose to have the transplant and went through the intake process to the program, the transplant program at Sunrise Hospital was shut down. This meant more stress: researching a new hospital, deciding upon Mayo Clinic, and traveling to and from Phoenix where it was located. Then, there was the screening process to find a donor match for my daughter and arranging for "Ant Lan's" help. The transplant team at the Mayo clinic assured us that the transplant was possible and that the complications would be minimal. However, our younger daughter was under intense medical supervision for months. She would also take anti-rejection medication for the remainder of her life.

Clearly, it was the most stressful situation in my life. When a parent has two children undergoing surgery simultaneously it is understandably stressful. I'm positive that my body and mind were pressured to their limits. Maria Shriver stated during her times of struggle, *"You have to be willing to let go of the life you planned in order to make the life you're meant to live."*[12] This was certainly true for our entire family during our daughter's transplant process. What I didn't realize is that I would have such a difficult time accepting this truth for myself.

My youngest daughter painfully and stoically accepted the realization that she would be classified as disabled for the rest of her life. She had envisioned additional education for herself along with a lifelong career. My older daughter who had donated the kidney, returned to her teaching career but with a keener focus on the fragility of everyday life. Even though I had finally reached the pinnacle of my nursing career, I adjusted my work schedule to accommodate my child's health care needs without reservation that any of my further career aspirations would suffer.

Stress indeed had physically affected my life more than I imagined. Within weeks of returning home from Phoenix, symptoms of my autoimmune diseases began to exacerbate. Performing my nursing duties and caring for my family exhausted me. My joints ached with every movement and every muscle tingled with torturous pain. It was clear that either I needed intense medication to calm my angry immune system or I needed to decrease the stress in my daily life, possibly both. Chemotherapy infusion treatments decreased the symptoms, but they also left me weak and nauseated. My medical specialist strongly advised me to decrease both my activity level and stress load in my workday. My doctor actually

---

[12] Grant, M. (2013) Finding the joy. AARP, Dec 2013/Jan2014, p. 41

stated that if I did not greatly decrease my stress level, my symptoms would kill me.

I approached my nursing supervisor, B[13] and advised her of my health status and my doctor's stern recommendation. I requested that I be assigned to a part-time nursing position within the Veteran's Administration. She curtly refused.

"There are no part-time nursing positions within the V.A. system," she stated with arrogance and suggested that I resign my position. She accused me of abandoning my patients and sabotaging her management position. She refused to help me navigate through the application process to apply for disability retirement. She also disrupted my disability retirement paperwork processing at the V.A. for a year. It was with great reluctance that I ended my full-time nursing duties while at the pinnacle of my career. I had devoted thirty years to my profession and had finely tuned my abilities. I achieved a Master's level in education; I felt confident about my professional talents and had achieved advanced certification in my career.

When the last day of work ended and I left my work area, no one bid me good- bye, no supervisor came to wish me well, no co-workers said farewell. No one acknowledged my presence or my leaving. I was certainly not ready to retire, and the absence of acknowledgement from my co-workers was an extra sting to my psyche.

A year later, I moved to Mississippi to deal with family issues. I immediately applied for a part-time nursing position with the local hospitals, clinics, and doctor's offices. I planned to continue to contribute to my profession by conducting chart reviews or performing case management duties. The response was, *"But you aren't from around here er ya?"* they said with a somewhat arrogant and biased attitude.

I didn't expect this response and couldn't understand what difference it made as to which part of the United States I had obtained my college degrees or in what regions of the country I had secured my nursing experience. After discussing my concern with my sisters (who are nurses), I soon discerned that it did indeed matter. I was not going to be considered for a nursing position in the South if I had been educated in the North. I naively thought that we had grown beyond that state of understanding. I

---

[13]   Not her real name.

173

was viewed as a Yankee and a carpet bagger. I still have a valid Mississippi nursing license, and I continue to pursue a part-time position but with the understanding that that goal will probably never be realized.

If only I had been able to work for a few more years while at the pinnacle of my nursing profession, enjoying robust health! I would have been able to make a noticeable contribution to the profession of nursing. I still mourn the death of my career. I try reimaging my life as I struggle through each infusion treatment. I, too, "kudda be'n sumbody". I can't help wondering how much more I could have contributed to the nursing profession if I could have had just a few more years to work. I miss it. I miss not being able to physically contribute.

****

Entertaining the vague desire to refocus my professional career began to entertain my thoughts. Realizing that I needed to recreate myself was the key. This process began by realizing that letting go of the image of myself was okay. This seemed to be the key for the transformation process. I had been a nurse for thirty years but I realized that was not who I was- it was what I had done as a profession. Any person who is going to be successful in changing careers or lifestyles, has to realize that the functions performed each day in the world are not who you are. They are merely duties for which you receive a paycheck.

It was then that I realized the most important aspect of the change process. It was obvious that I had put a great effort into planning for my life as a nurse— studying in the library, developing patient care plans, studying disease processes of major illnesses until I knew them by heart. I could recite patient safety policy and procedures from memory. Nurse managers had consulted me when questions of care or issues of disease contamination needed to be resolved. I was considered an expert in my professional field.

However, I had not studied, planned for or developed a strategy for myself after my nursing career. This was a critical issue. It seemed to be the obvious thing to do, but it had not occurred to me until I was faced with it. So, I went back to the drawing board using the same tools that had worked for me when I began my nursing career. I looked within myself.

Deciding what I needed to do to get my nursing degree required sifting through each and every step I would need to take. First, I had to have that all-important talk with myself. Did I have the guts to go to school, raise a family, and work while going to school? Most women find being a military wife a full-time job in itself, so this was an important question to answer. I would be taking on three or four full- time jobs. Could I do it? I decided that I could. I started when my third child was only six weeks old.

A person doesn't truly know what they are made of unless they try something that they yearn to do. The fire in my belly motivated me to become a nurse. I believed that I could go to school, graduate, obtain a nursing license and have a professional career. Trying made it possible. I just developed a path that appeared to be correct and kept going forward. Reaching my professional goal was its own reward.

The person you are comes from the essence of yourself. It's the thoughts and feelings that circulate within you each day. The accumulation of the decisions that a person makes each time he or she encounters situations set the stage for the next decision. Letting go of the previous me was a psychologically process: one that occurred in my spirit and my mind. Relieving myself of the idea of the previous me left an open area to fill up with new ideas and a new person.

This was an extremely difficult and uncomfortable process and for me. I had spent a tremendous amount of time, money, and effort in being who I was and in doing what I did. I knew this area. I had settled into a routine. Things were known. Things were comfortable. No person in their right mind would want to willfully leave a profession or lifestyle that they were comfortable with or one where they could easily use their natural talents effortlessly; especially if the person had spent a reasonable amount of time developing those talents.

This filling up process was and is very important. It is an on-going endeavor. It begins by understanding it. Like all processes, the new me occurred in stages. Re- imagining yourself can also be a scary issue. People generally don't like or lean easily toward change. We are all creatures of habit. So when we are faced with rearranging our basic selves from head to toe it's obvious that we will need to take a hard look at ourselves, inside out. A person becomes vulnerable during this process. You must be willing to and brave enough to strip all of your outside crap away that you show to the world.

It's important to sort through positive talents that you currently have and find the positive qualities that you have carried with you through your life. They obviously have aided you. Your positive qualities may be your sense of humor or your ability to look at the world pleasantly. Both of these abilities will aid you in whatever you chose to do next on your other life path.

However, there are probably a lot of other negative or useless talents or abilities that I possess that I have been carrying around with me for years. These may be as simple as my preference for using bad avenues to express my best qualities. This is a great time to get rid of them. They don't work. Yeah! Trash time…

So when, I realized that the old me is no longer relevant, I started to rid myself of unneeded abilities. Now, the re-creation process begins. Possibly the best manner in which to do this is to spend some time determining what abilities wanted to develop within myself when I was younger but didn't have time. Maybe I spent too much time at work or had too many family duties that required your attention. Possibly I needed to concentrate on your job to make sure that you made the correct decision to advance your career. I wanted to advance in my profession and secure an income for my family's future. Maybe I needed to care for a family member who was disabled or dying of a terminal illness. This could easily require full-time attention. Many middle aged adults find themselves sandwiched in between caring for their children while caring for aging parents simultaneously.

Well, I had filled my early adult and middle-aged years working in the nursing profession and caring for my husband and children. It was obvious that my career was over, my children were now grown adults, and my first husband had deceived me and was now deceased.

Examining my options was both enjoyable and painful. When I started thinking about the things I enjoyed as a teen, I realized that my life had been so filled with activities for the past few years that my recollection was clouded with memories and recent career projects. I had to work hard to have these issues fade from my mind. Once this was completed, I focused on going forward with my new life: my new self.

Re-imagining my new self, required that I focus on me. There were no small children in my life who needed nurturing, no work schedules that were tempting my time, no professional ladder to climb. The key was to look at the inner me and ask - *what would I like to do?* The answers came slowly – but they had been waiting for a very long time.

The talent of gardening and nurturing plants came to the surface first. I enjoy putting a living plant in the earth, nourishing it, and watching it grow. I began attending local gardening club meetings. I discovered which plants grew best in my neighborhood. I studied and learned the names of plants I didn't recognize. Quickly, I collected and planted a new variety of specimens in my back yard that thrived. This offered me a metaphor. If the plants could grow in their new environment, then I knew that I could also grow in my new re-imagined life.

Enjoying time with my extended family and gleaning joy from those simple activities was its own reward. That is when I knew that I had a grip on my new life: when I could take pleasure in my new activities. I could now enjoy taking time to plant flowers and plants and not worry about what else I should be doing instead of enjoying the growth of nature. I had made the transition.

Now, I'm busy filling up my new lifestyle with my new life. Taking pleasure in watching a beautiful flower unfold its petals is a wonderful process. The flower is much like me as I'm unfolding the sections of my new life. The quest of being somebody has helped me process into my new lifestyle. The disillusionment felt by Marlon Brando haunted me – but only for a small moment. However, I didn't make the transition until I was forced into it. Waiting a few more years would have been my choice before making the re-imagining. But we never know what's around the corner. I am somebody and am slowly and surely becoming the person I was meant to be at this point in my life. It fits me very well. I surely have *listened to the "lines"* of communication in my life and realize that I have formed my own person and take joy from who I have become. It is important for each of us to remember that we influence people in our lives. They are "listening" to us in our daily lives. These tid bits of listening that others hear form "lines" of communication which help to mold a person's essence.

Remember, each of us is helping to form another person. Each of us is creating and composing a line which will be listened to by others. How will you sound when someone listens to you? What will the line look like that connects you to another person? Will it be made of hearts and hugs or arrows and sorrows?

Printed in the United States
By Bookmasters